DEDICATION

Dedicated to my loving husband, Gene, with whom I shared the ministry and who unceasingly encouraged me to write about our exciting jungle ministry, to my three wonderful children, Joy, Steve and Patricia, who sacrificed a great deal so that we could remain there and share the Gospel and lastly, to tens of thousands of friends and pastors who prayed for us, supported us and encouraged us through difficult times. To all, I owe my deepest gratitude and love.

Sandy Thomas

THE REPUBLIC OF CONGO

AREA
132,046 square miles (slightly larger than New Mexico) and situated northwest of the Democratic Republic of the Congo, formerly Zaire, and south of the Central African Republic

PEOPLE
Nine major ethnic groups of the Bantu family of languages, plus 70 sub-groups and also several Pygmy groups with similar tongues

POPULATION
2.5 million to 3 million people

RELIGIONS
Indigenous/animist +35%, Roman
Catholic 41%, Protestants 20%, other, (cults, Muslims, etc.) +4%

POLITICS
Independent of France since 1960. A one party Marxist oriented system was denounced in February 1991 and a change to a multi party democratic form of government was approved. Elections were held in 1992. This government continued until 1998 when the former Marxist regime overthrew the democratic government in a coup. During this brief time, between 1994 and 1998, there was an ethnic war and a civil war resulting in the death of tens of thousands of people. Many Congolese migrated to other African countries as the capital was being shelled and partially destroyed. This resulted in the evacuation of most of the missionary force and foreign diplomats. The country is still under military control unless free elections are allowed at some future date.

ECONOMY
Congo is considered a lower income country with a per capita of $1,230. The country exports petroleum, high quality lumber of redwood, coca and coffee beans as well as other minerals. Congo has the most petroleum offshore south of the Sahara Desert, but a large debt with the World Bank and the IMF cripples the recovery to a good, stable economy. This is due in part to wars, tribal conflicts and bad management.

TABLE OF CONTENTS

INTRODUCTION

Sandy Thomas was born Madelyn Wacker, in Bloom City, Wisconsin. Her parents were Robert and Ella Wacker, her father being deceased. She graduated from Beloit Memorial High school in Beloit, Wisconsin. She is an alumni of Columbia International University in Columbia, South Carolina. She and her husband, Gene, went to France for language study in 1954 and on to the Republic of Congo in 1955. Mrs. Thomas is a registered Red Cross nurse, having been trained in the Congo to perform many procedures that included diagnosing illnesses, dispensing medication, suturing up all minor and major cuts, helping with surgery at the local hospital, and performing amputations on the lepers and skin grafts on those who had long term ulcerous sores. On long extended river trips, traveling in a dugout canoe, thousands were treated for yaws disease. Mrs. Thomas worked with the Government in controlling yaws, leprosy and in the immunization programs. This program she spearheaded to save thousands of children from certain death. She was named to the General Assembly to be a representative of the International Red Cross. Her ministry and that of her husband were intertwined to use all measures available to them to be ambassadors of the Lord Jesus Christ. She and her husband have been retired since July of 1997. They now travel to various churches throughout the U.S. to tell their story of God's mercies in the Congo. Mrs. Thomas will continue to write of their life beyond the jungle walls of the Congo, a life filled with excitement, trials, fears, tears and much joy. Rev. and Mrs. Thomas and their three grown children are living proof of God's power in their lives. It is her hope that these true life stories will challenge young people to go forth to fill the gap of retired missionaries and that others will be challenged to try God and find that He will meet all life's challenges.

After Bible college studies were terminated in 1954, Gene and Sandy went to Paris, France for advanced French studies beyond that which they had had in college. They arrived in the Republic of Congo, then known as Equatorial Africa, in July of 1955. Forty two years of ministry, that began as a pioneer work, began to come into focus in this rather obscure area of the world about a degree and a half above the equator. Few people were familiar at that time and even today with this small country that was a former French colony.

The mission station was given to United World Mission by the local tribal chiefs. There seemed to be plenty of land wrapped up in a thick jungle setting, but there were no permanent buildings in which to live. Living in mud houses for a term, while building brick homes later was a chapter of great tenacity in enduring the day to day living in a strange and peculiar society. Daily living was a formidable challenge in itself. What lay ahead was even a greater challenge as they made plans to teach thousands of people to read and write. There were no pastors and if the work were to grow, a Bible school was needed to train young men to be the spiritual leaders of their own people. Many rivers crisscrossed the great area of the northern territories and much evangelism was needed to reach the unreached with the Gospel way back in the deepest jungles. At some point, there was an enormous need for good medical care for the area but that would wait years before that dream was realized. Sandwiched in between was the raising of a family of three children that God entrusted to them. Each segment of the work, be it for the ministry or for them personally, would challenge every ounce of their energies and their desires to remain faithful to an unfailing God.

Their forty-two years of ministry tested the validity of God's Word and the power of God to keep them in the face of extreme dangers, tropical diseases and raising children in this setting. Their faith WAS tested. Would they remain faithful and could they carry out the Great Commission that they had been challenged to carry? This book is a collection of stories with the background being the large area where they served. The northern part of the Republic of Congo has never been fully mapped out due to the region being mostly swamps, jungle trees growing out of the water and small rivers passing through the jungles. Explorers have died there in an effort to track unknown animals. No other American missions resided in northern Congo during their years on the field. The Thomas' are the only white people alive today who have the history on this part of Congo Brazzaville.

It is their desire that this book will challenge all people, but especially young people, with the task that is yet before them to carry the news of the Gospel to the ends of the earth. No matter how difficult the country might be, how strange the languages, God is able to help the worker overcome all problems to establish a national church that will remain long after the missionary has gone.

In their travels across the United States, they have been asked to tell their stories of life as they knew it in the rugged jungles of northern Congo. They are stories that will leave a lasting impression on all those who hear. No one remains the same after listening to how God kept them through long years of Communism, being on hit lists to be murdered, and living through many conflicts as well as an ethnic war during their last term of service in the capital city of Brazzaville. As the shells burst all around them and the tanks lurked like huge beasts in the shadows of deserted streets at night, they were safe in the knowledge that God was right beside them. God has now given them time to tell their story and they trust to be able, in the years ahead of them, to publish more about the exciting and sometimes frightening experiences that God took them through to help build His Church.

The Great World Tragedy

Today, the people of God, are looking at a world torn apart by hate and greed, a world suffering from the most catastrophic disasters known to man. The Thomas' adopted country, the Republic of Congo-Brazzaville, agonized through ethnic and civil wars in the nineties, leaving countless thousands dead, maimed and displaced to other countries as refugees, people without identity and without hope.

As the Republic of Congo-Brazzaville endeavors to repair the small former French colony, their eyes are fixed upon another tragedy. Separated by the great Congo River, the people are hearing and reliving the sounds of guns and death. Relatives and friends have been fleeing the Democratic Republic of the Congo-Kinshasa, formerly Belgian Congo and Zaire.

Hundreds of thousands flee to the forest where they die of starvation, malaria and dysentery. Thousands more cross the Ubangui River to their area, in the north, Impfondo, the region of the Likouala.

Dr. Joseph Harvey, his colleagues and the United Nations help minister to the people's needs the best they can. Without access to large food and medical supplies, the suffering is intolerable.

The Democratic Republic of the Congo-Kinshasa is decimated from the north to the south. Rebels roaming the country steal what they want and kill at random. Children, by the thousands are orphans, starving and ill. Recent United Nation atrocities show people from more educated countries making prostitutes from little girls.

They have no voice, no home and no one who cares. A population is weeping, screaming in despair and their feeble cries are silenced by the evils of man and the liberal news media.

In December, 2004, the giant waves of the Tsunami flashed around the world. They even reached the shores of war torn Africa. People responded by sending hundreds of millions of dollars and they gathered thousands of tons of food. Yet, when the ragged, hungry and gaunt faces of little children stood looking at officials on the evening news, their hearts hoped for help—help in the way they needed never really arrived. Yes, the eyes of the Universe looked on and then turned away. Their sad eyes tore at our heartstrings. Sometimes at night, We heard their voices. We saw the tears rolling down dirty little cheeks covered with flies. We visited their sick in our dreams. They are still there today, standing and waiting.

The rich resources of this once beautiful land have been stolen away. The greatest resource, its peoples, have now had their lives shattered and their dignity taken away.

The focus of America must take a second look at another kind of Tsunami, one in which there is a daily wave of the destruction of a nation and a great part of its continent.

The great missionary, Livingston, gazed upon a people steeped in idol worship and fetishes. He looked beyond, also and envisioned a Church made up of the same people. He must have peered down the corridors of time to see the change that the Gospel of Christ would bring someday.

Hidden in the forest, the villages and the once modern cities, is the Church that Christ built. It has been trodden down and wounded, but it is still alive and hopeful that somewhere, somehow, Christian brothers and sisters in America might give a helping hand to this area of Africa, and much more—a cup of cold water in Jesus name.

The Psalmist David sang in Psalm 65:5,6,7,8:

You answer us with awesome deeds of righteousness, O God our Savior, the hope of all the ends of the earth and of the farthest seas, who formed the mountains by your power, having armed yourself with strength, who stilled the roaring of the seas, the roaring of their waves, and the turmoil of the nations. Those living far away fear your wonders; where morning dawns and evening fades, you call forth songs of joy.

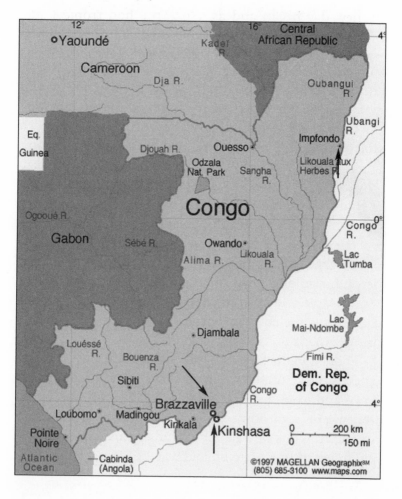

TRACING THE LONG JOURNEY

A new day began and as usual, the hot, tropical sun effortlessly pierced the smog to steam the busy city.

Cathedral of Notre Dame

Close to the streets, a thick yellow carpet of car fumes and dust covered the people as they scurried about their business. Street vendors sold everything from fruits and vegetables to stolen clothes, watches, and a vast array of many other things that had been taken from stores, homes or the airport customs warehouses. At times, it seemed that there were more selling items of one nature or another on the streets than those in the stores. The year was 1955 and we had finally arrived in the small, colonized country of Congo. This was a part of French Equatorial Africa. We had waited so long for this moment and now it had become a reality.

Coming this far had not been without incident. In 1954, we joined a large group of anxious students from Columbia Bible College in Columbia, South Carolina, that was headed for some distant shores in far away lands.

13

Many from our class would carry the Good News of Salvation to people who had never before heard. All of us had been trained to go, not counting the cost, that we might be a part of the Great Commission as given in the last verses of Matthew.

The obstacles of French language study in Paris, France were numerous. If we thought that we had suffered while working our way through college, we were about to embrace a whole new way of life and culture. West Europe was very foreign to us as American students. Europe was still reeling from the effects of World War II. Signs of that conflict were everywhere. The ancient building that housed our apartment was home to a Protestant family. Unfortunately, they were located many stories up. We walked up and down the one hundred twenty steps two to three times a day. The ray of joy in this daily act was walking out of the dark, gray stone of the inner courtyard and looking out to the beautiful Cathedral of Notre Dame along the Seine River.

We had read romantic stories of the beauty of Paris,

Sandy in Paris, France

but we saw little of that side of this historic city. People everywhere appeared to be walking in a daze. No one laughed. Everyone looked as if they were carrying some inner weight, some struggle, some heartache. Deep lines etched the faces of the masses. Many had become old before his or her time. It was a city without a ray of hope. Our extremely meager salary was not sufficient to pay for subway tickets, so we walked miles to our French classes at the Alliance Francaise. Hunger seemed to stalk us like

A homeless man in Paris

an uninvited guest, hunger that was eating away at our already thin frames. Lessons for our future ministry were going to be learned right here on a daily basis. Before our Bible college days, we had experienced great abundance. Now, we were going to experience want and often despair.

Summer had turned to Fall and the apartment on the top floor was dark and cold. Before the winter was over, I came down with pneumonia. Deep within me, I was wondering if all this was worth the effort. Few people had sufficient funds to turn the heat on before the first of December. It was not uncommon to wear more than one layer of clothing. Lessons were learned in a hurry to wear gloves and a heavy winter coat in our apartment in order to conserve body heat. Taking a bath under these conditions was very difficult to say the least.

Trying to study our lessons was very stressful and this was a factor that would challenge our call from God. It became evident to us that our teachers, and most other people around us had only two changes of clothing for a whole year. The Second World War was over, but the suffering and deprivation were still ongoing. The children played in the courtyards and magically learned how to escape the memories of a tragic war. The adults moved about in morbid silence, thinking only of getting through another day. Under the city bridges lived another group of people, the forgotten ones of war. There, the homeless lived and died. Some moved about the city pushing an old broken baby buggy piled high with rags and half empty wine bottles. No jesting and smiles came from these nameless people. This was a people who had suffered too much and too long. Their haggard faces and emaciated bodies told the whole story. If only Jesus could come and give them hope.

After a year of study and suffering, in our private way, we understood in some small way, the plight of the masses that made up the countries of Western Europe. For all these people, nothing would ever erase the symbols of a horrific war. The people became the tragic pictures of pain and this pain would be forever engraved on the hearts of all who had experienced the bombs and starvation.

Winter turned into a beautiful Spring in Paris. We finally left the dismal apartment in Paris and rented a small place in the suburbs where living was much cheaper. We took an electric train to and from the city each day. We could then see the famous flower gardens of the city that were in full bloom. Often, we walked through the unusually designed gardens and savored the sweet smells and beauty that gave promise of a new life, a life that differed so greatly from the life outside the garden walls. Living in the countryside helped us to save money so that we could vacation in other parts of Europe. There we got a better perspective on the ravages of war. We walked among the ruins of bombed out factories and homes. We could little imagine though what these people had suffered.

The craters and devastation were all around us, but in the midst of that ruin and scenes of decay were the wild flowers springing up. It was like a sign, that out of the embers of fire and destruction, there would be new life. New homes and office buildings were being built, with the Marshall Plan, alongside the bombed out structures of gray steel. A very small glimmer of hope was everywhere since the American aid money was being poured into the building of a new era. From the ashes came the hope for a better future, maybe, just maybe, one without another war like that one. These experiences of travel made a profound impression on our lives. We needed to see and smell the changes. We were being allowed to look inside the deep recesses of the hearts of suffering mankind. So long our own little world in the United States had been far removed from all this day to day struggle. We had heard so much back home, but we felt so little sympathy, until now. We were young and there was so much to learn. Time was on our side. Saying goodbye to Paris was not difficult. Nothing there had drawn us to their hopeless way of life. Long, thin bread and a bottle of wine came to be the symbol of French life at that time. It was easy to go and not look back.

Missionary friends accompanied us to the train. A night sleeper would take us to Marseille in southern France. There we would spend a few days of sightseeing before boarding a French "paqueboat" that would allow us to see many African cities on the coast before arriving at Congo's port city of Point Noire that was on the edge of the Atlantic Ocean. After twenty-one days of ocean travel, visiting the various coastal cities and suffering extreme bouts of sea-sickness, we were glad to see the Congo coastline come into view.

Another train ride on the night express took us from

the busy and boisterous life of Pointe Noire to the capital city of Brazzaville. The train screeched and rumbled as it ambled its way toward the countryside. The moonlight outlined the forms of wild animals eating vegetation on the nearby hills. Although we had our own cabin, we were often reminded throughout the night that hundreds of people were jammed into the corridors with their tied up sheep and baskets of squawking chickens. The night passed slowly as the rickety train squeaked and jerked by the sleeping villages. One look at the crooked tracks made us wonder how we could possibly arrive safely at our destination. The fact that we did was a complete miracle to us.

The sun was rising too quickly. Our weary bodies didn't want to respond to the day that awaited us. The bunks were made of metal and they surely didn't afford any comfort for sleeping. Leaving them would bring no remorse. The train sluggishly squealed into the Brazzaville train station. Seemingly, the whole population of the city was there, either to greet family members or to watch friends and relatives depart on the return trip. We scanned the vast crowd hoping to see someone who would look like a foreign missionary. We prayed that someone would spot us. We were both ill and could not afford to stand long in the intense heat and humidity. Being the only whites on board, it was not difficult for the Swedish missionaries to pick us out of the masses. How beautiful it is to be recognized in a far away place when you know no one!

A young Swedish doctor drove us to the Swedish Mission in the middle of the city. Having lost twenty more pounds on the voyage down, the perceiving eyes of the young physician noted that I needed quick medical care. Not wanting to wait another minute, he called the French hospital to talk with a French doctor. He suggested that we waste no time in being treated. The trip to the hospital was only minutes along a beautiful boulevard. We were soon diagnosed with malaria and I was found to be three months pregnant. I was placed in the maternity ward where I found a nice bed that had crisp, white sheets. Nurses were quickly summoned to give injections to stem the vomiting and the malaria. The twenty-one days on the ship had taken their toll. Suffering from dehydration and great weight loss, there was a great chance that I would miscarry the baby that I did not know I was carrying. At that moment, there was a strong desire to cry and be safe at home in America. I was over-whelmed by my physical condition.

My husband, Gene, who was present, looked on with a very white face. He, too, was becoming more ill as each hour passed. The doctor, knowing the seriousness of our malaria, needed to treat us aggressively and immediately, so he put Gene in the bed next to me. That doctor will never know the peace that I felt and the comfort knowing that my husband was right by my side. He made a comment that they had never had a male in the maternity ward before. I was too ill to appreciate the humor until many days later.

This was our entrance into Congo and a reminder that God had chosen us to come to this Third World country that would prove to be harsh on health and per-ilous to living. The experiences of our arrival would not soon be forgotten. Although we did not voice our thoughts of going back home, we did check out our rea-sons for coming to Africa. We needed to verify with God again and again our future intentions to serve Him in this land. God was taking us one step at a time, and it seemed that there was trouble on every hand. God didn't leave us without a message through these times of speculation. Over and over He was whispering the words of the

Psalmist, "For in the time of trouble He shall hide me in His pavilion: in the secret of His tabernacle shall He hide me; He shall set me up upon a rock" (Psalm 27:5).

After several weeks of treatment and excellent meals at the hospital, we regained some of our strength again. We began preparations for flying north to our jungle station at Impfondo. We bought cases of canned foods and other dry food supplies to help us in the months ahead. Our wonderful Heavenly Father was making us ready to leave the security and safety net of the Swedish Mission.

It wasn't possible for anyone to really prepare us for our unusual future life in the isolated jungles of the Likouala Region. However, our all-knowing Father had not left us to ourselves. A few years prior to our leaving the shores of America, God had given us a gift in the form of a verse that we could carry with us the rest of our life. The beautiful nuggets were tucked away in Proverbs 3:5,6. "Trust in the Lord with all thine heart; and lean not unto thine own understanding. In all thy ways acknowledge Him, and He shall direct thy paths." Perspiration beaded our faces as we rode to the Brazzaville airport that was several miles from the Swedish Mission. We presented our tickets and a fine young Frenchman led us onto the airstrip. We looked at the old World War II plane and wondered how trustworthy it would be for the four and a half hour flight over the lush jungle some six hundred and fifty miles to the far north. Our destination was to a place we had never seen, except by pictures. We would soon meet a people we had never known. Our home was to be extremely primitive, to say the least. Living was going to be very difficult and dangers would abound all around us. Was God sure that He really wanted us in such a place? The comforts of a modern world were now behind us. We were venturing into a new and strange culture, a lifestyle that even the most active mind could not conceive of. We had, at last, come face to face with the real calling of God, the stark reality of what we had promised God that we would do if He would walk with us. Our lives had been set apart years prior to this important day.

The French copilot finally closed the steel door of the plane and we swayed and bumped down the runway on our way to a little known grassy airstrip somewhere in the Congo forest. As the plane creaked and lumbered its way into the atmosphere, we settled back in our uncomfortable steel seats. We both stared out the window and wondered about the realities of all our many tomorrows. Gene looked at me reassuringly and I found comfort in his smile. Since this old relic of a warplane had been in use for a very long time, I could intelligently guess that the much used motors could possibly give us some trouble. But why worry now? We were on our way. I have a very vivid imagination but I was not imagining that the motors sounded strange. They were making grinding sounds that were all too real and a tinge of fear came over my already anxious heart. The noise made it impossible to carry on a conversation so we spoke to one another with our eyes. To add to the uncertainty of our situation, one of the motors appeared to be spewing out streams of fire from time to time.

The pilot turned often to check his two passengers. We were the only ones and that alone seemed strange. Was that place so bad that no one wanted to go there? The pilot, noticing our apprehension, quickly assured us that his "baby" often acted in this manner. There was no cause for alarm. Those words meant little to me as I watched those troublesome motors. Looking below brought even less comfort. We had left the familiar scenery of the high, barren hills around the capital city. They were replaced by a carpet of beautiful, thick jungle. As far as the eye could see, the jungles stretched to the distant horizons. Who could ever penetrate such a vast and fearful place? Snaking its way through this maze of heavy foliage was the Congo River that farther up river branched off into the old Belgian Congo, now known as the Democratic Republic of Congo. As the Congo River turned to the northeast, the Ubanghi River went on to its final destination in the Central African Republic.

Heavy jungles are known to create much turbulence when flying over them, and without a doubt, we seemed to be bouncing all over the sky. Waves of nausea came over me and gripped my whole being. I was handed a large can and it was put to use in a hurry. The excitement of this trip had worn off already. Without warning, the plane shook violently as it began to descend into the thick cloud cover. To our amazement, a rather large village came into view and instantly, I felt knots in my stomach. Little could we know that this unique place was going to be "home" for thirty-eight of our forty-two years. The plane lined up in front of a long, grassy runway. We were skipping over the landing area before coming to a full stop in the mud. All along the strip were lines of black, shiny bodies. A strange feeling of love engulfed me. These were going to be our people, our family. The pilot opened the door and we looked out to waiting missionary co-workers, Betty Sadler and Mrs. Verna Sigler.

As we carefully made our way down the narrow steps, we both knew that the long journey was over. God's work for us was just beginning. Little could we know the hardships that we would face or the dangerous encounters that we would experience. In the end, our very faith would be tested and we would find out who God really is, how He provides and how great is His power to those who will dare believe Him for His very Word's sake.

THE BIG MUD HOUSE

After leaving the grassy runway, we drove through the village in a government truck that the two resident lady missionaries had been able to obtain. People were lined up along the dirt road to catch a glimpse of the newcomers. We had mixed emotions about this event and were anxious to get settled in. On one side of us was the great Ubanghi River and on the other side was the village. Not too far back of the many mud huts was the thick jungle that extended all the way to the Cameroon border. It

Mud house where we lived for 4 years

was a frightening thought as I pondered the distances. Suddenly, we turned into a well-kept yard with palm trees everywhere.

We saw a row of beautiful bushes on each side of the wide path leading to the house. This gave the mud house personality. An announcement was made that we were "home." No amount of previous descriptions could have prepared us for this momentous event. The mud walls had been whitewashed to make it more presentable, but the dirt floors inside were just that, DIRT. Since we were going to have a little one come into the home in the

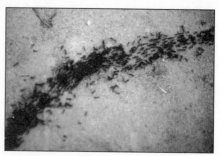

Trail of soldier and driver ants

months that followed, I couldn't help but think about all the hazards and daily conditions that we would experience.

The bamboo roof had holes in it and the space between the roofing poles and the mud walls made large openings for creatures of many kinds to climb over. In a sense, no one could have described to us this strange way of living. The weeks and months began to pass quickly and we were getting used to our new surroundings. Daylight hours brought wonderful, new experiences for us. However, I was never comfortable when night fell at six each evening. There were no city lights anywhere, just the flicker of the pressure lantern against the mud walls.

The outside brought out its array of croaks, buzzing, splashing in the river and the ever vigilant songs of the night birds. Eerie shadows were cast on the walls. Chills ran up and down my spine as I thought of the snakes in the trees and the leopards that prowled outside. We were so close to the river that we could hear the bellowing of the large crocodiles. The jungle sounds wanted to terrorize me and sleep didn't come easily. Large driver ants or soldier ants, as they are often called, were out in the area scouting every area of the mission station. We had read the horror stories of these ants attacking helpless animals and even people. We were told early on that when they invaded a house, be it in the daytime or during the night, the occupants should leave immediately. After they would kill and carry away their prey, that included lizards, cockroaches, mice, chickens in the hen house, or other small things, they would form a line and leave. We found this story to be quite accurate—frightening.

Young Congolese had been hired to cut the grass on a continuous basis. This was done in order to keep the snakes from hiding in the tall grass. Believe me, they were there and a great menace to all. Even with constant vigil, snakes would appear from nowhere. After dark, we went out to the hen house to close the door for the night. Gene would flash the beam of the flashlight outside the chicken coup. Every night we would see the glow of the eyes of wild animals on the edge of the jungle. It didn't take long for questions to arise in my heart. Was I ready to spend a lifetime in this forsaken part of the world? Could I raise a family here? Ultimately, was fear going to rule me and be my constant partner? Would we learn the language? How on earth could we understand what the people were saying to us? We knew it was absolutely necessary to learn their tongue if we wanted to carry the Gospel.

We had had three years of French but that seemed all but useless in this place where the forest people spoke a strange language called Lingala. The village children were taught French in the schools, but as soon as they ran out the doors for home, they spoke in the Lingala language. However long it would take us, we would set our hearts to learning. Having settled the problem in our hearts, we set about learning phrase structure, thousands of vocabulary words and finally using what we were learning from the Lingala lessons and books. As we look back on that time, with all its uncertainties, we know that those thoughts were normal. The God who had called us would prepare us both for the years of ministry that stretched out before us. As we read God's Word and prayed daily, it was apparent that He who had called us would also prepare us and teach us in the way that we should go.

The training period begins

The training period had really begun a few years earlier in 1951 when we had entered Columbia Bible College. We arrived at college with a burning desire in our hearts to train for missionary work. There was a deep conviction within us that God was calling us for a lifetime of service. We knew that nothing was going to hinder us from fulfilling that call if we followed in the footsteps of our Lord. Day after day, we sat under Godly professors who expounded on the Word of God. Our souls absorbed the wonderful teachings as if we were sponges. Every week, the teachers were challenging us to offer ourselves as instruments to God that He might take us to win a lost world. Missionary speakers returned from the ends of the earth and spoke of the need to venture into wild jungles, travel hidden waterways and trek unknown paths of the world in an effort to seek out the lost ones for our Lord. Time was given to us for long periods of soul searching. Together, we set our eyes on the goal before us and there would be no turning back. It was time to give our youth and our very lives to fulfill His will.

As we pondered these unusual life-changing ideas, our first major lesson of total surrender was about to begin. God was taking us at our word.

It was an unusually cold January day for South

Carolina and I was not feeling very well. My husband, Gene, told me to stay in bed for the rest of the day. He would go to class alone that day. Before his departure, I asked that he fill the pot bellied stove with more coal to warm up the small second floor apartment. Before going down the outside stairs of the old wooden house, he kissed me and hurried away. The chill seemed penetrating so I pulled the covers over my head and fell into a deep sleep. Somewhere in my dreams, I heard someone calling my name and screaming, "Sandy, get out, the house is on fire."

There was such urgency in the voice that I threw back the covers and sat upright. Fire had burned through the ceiling in our bedroom and flames were licking at the upper section of my bed. I ran to the kitchen door that seemed to be banging back and forth. I peered into an inferno of flames that engulfed the large kitchen area. The windows were breaking all around and falling into the alley below. They sounded like popcorn as they exploded. Terrified, I ran to the closet to retrieve our

Village along the Impfondo Road

clothes. There was no way to get them out. It was an old fashioned closet with some hooks one direction and the others the opposite direction. The flames blew at me. I didn't want to leave. We had so little but what we had was priceless. There was the wedding album, the book of poetry that as yet had not been published. Other gifts were now in smoke—lost forever. I stood for an instant and gazed at our earthly possessions. Fire was surrounding me fast and if I was to survive, I needed to move quickly. Time had run out. Barefoot and wearing only light pajamas, I slipped down the back fire escape. With hot tears coursing down my cheeks, I fled along the narrow alley-way. All that we owned had disappeared in a flash of fire.

At college, my husband received word, in one of his classes, that our apartment had burned and he was needed immediately back home. Frantically, he got into the car and sped back to what had been our home. Fire engines were arriving and going to work quickly to prevent the blaze from spreading to adjacent homes that were built with wood. Running through the crowd, he came upon me. We cried together. He had visions of me perishing in the blaze. The bottom part of the four apartment building was saved, although greatly damaged by smoke and fire. The situation seemed so hopeless. The days that followed were days of soul searching as we sought to find answers for the tragedy that had befallen us. If we had entertained the idea that God had forsaken us, it was all dispelled when the evening papers were put on the news stands later that day. We were identified and the tragic story of our loss was spelled out in detail.

No one ever knew the real story of what happened. An army couple shared our kitchen at the apartment and a back bedroom. We went to thank the young woman some days later for calling my name and screaming for me to leave as fire had engulfed the place. She looked at us in a questioning way. She stated that she had not called me because she knew that I went to school every morning and would have had no idea that I was in bed asleep. It took some time for us to understand all this. If she had not called me, who did? God had entered my dream that morning and allowed me to hear those terrifying words, "Sandy, get out, the house is on fire." God was there all the time. I had not been alone.

Prior to the fire, we had desperately sought the Lord's face that He might supply some four hundred dollars that we needed to make the final payment on our new car. We had also prayed for funds to buy an accordion to be used for our ministry in Africa. Money was tight as Gene was only able to work on weekends and that was not sufficient to pay bills, let alone buy the things that we felt we needed. At the time that we prayed, we had no idea how God would work it all out. We realized later that God's ways are far above our ways. He had allowed everything that we owned to be taken away so that He might show us His great power in providing again all that we needed and so much more.

Were we prepared and ready to leave for the mission field now that we had experienced some hard times? Surely, we had learned to rely solely on Him. No, the lessons that our Heavenly Father wanted us to learn were just the beginning. We had left a high paying job at the Ford Motor Company. All that we had saved was gone. A weekend job at the meat market didn't stretch very far. But God knew how to work through those problems. The man who was store manager was not a Christian but God used him in a most unusual way. He undoubtedly observed how thin we were and quietly went about helping us in a very constructive way. Each Saturday night he would give us two of each cut of meat and fish that would last for the next seven days. At a place called the "Barn," we were able to buy canned fruits, vegetables and soups for about one dollar a basket. They had been bought from stores where fire and water had taken off the labels. It was always a surprise as to what we were opening, but we were grateful for the day to day way our Heavenly Father met our needs. At an egg farm, we bought eggs for almost nothing. These were candled eggs that were cracked and could not be sold in the stores. We became convinced that the lady was so sorry for us that she actually cracked the eggs for us. They were always the largest of the eggs. Without realizing it, we were anticipating the way that God would meet our daily needs. There were bills to be paid, such as health insurance and utility bills.

Our fifteen dollar a week income was not sufficient to pay for all that and groceries, too. As we earnestly sought God's face, He was speaking to hearts in distant cities to have a part in our training for Africa. God knows all those dear people who gave time and again that we might receive the best training possible for our future ministry. Rewards will be given out some day for all the faithful servants who helped us in significant ways. Most of the time, we never knew where the money was coming from to meet our needs, but God made sure that it was there. Sometimes there was money in the mail; sometimes there was just an unsigned envelope in our school box with money in it. Our faith increased by leaps and bounds. We knew that God's hand was upon us for His work in Africa and whatever came into our life, He would never leave us nor forsake us. The Great Provider was our daily companion.

Shocked back to reality, we braced ourselves for this new life and prayed that we would not fail in all that the Lord had commissioned us to do. It was good to learn early that what we faced was greater than we were and that there was no way that we would accomplish anything lasting without supernatural guidance.

Even as I assessed my surroundings with all the dangers, deep in my heart I was thinking that my husband would always be there for me. He would comfort and protect me in the face of any unforeseen and life threatening situation. My schooling would be an ongoing process as I had not learned the most important lesson that God wanted me to learn. I had yet to discover the meaning of total trust in God at all times.

We were living in the far north of Congo, about a degree and a half above the equator. There were two seasons that included a heavy rainy season and a dry season. The rainy season was characterized by some 200-400 inches of rain a year that caused the Ubanghi River to rise and fall some twenty to thirty feet. The dry season gave forth no rain. The ground became parched and cracked. The heat and high humidity caused the trees to drip much moisture most of the time. This was typical jungle land. At times, we felt that the heat was unbearable and more than we could take. Yet, our Lord's Grace was all sufficient for these times of extreme discomfort. The 55,000 square miles of Northern Congo were a veritable river and swampland.

Most of the people lived along the hundreds of miles of waterways and made a living by making small gardens of maniac, plantain bananas, regular eating bananas, various greens like collards, pineapples, guavas, mangoes, oranges, grapefruit, papayas, avocados and field corn. Fishing and hunting were the main tasks that fell to the men folk. As I observed the men in their dugout canoes and the women going to their jungle gardens every day, I could see that they were at peace and happy. I really needed to be courageous, as they were, in order to survive the hostile environment in which we found ourselves.

On one Friday evening, we sat in the large kitchen playing some games. The rain was pounding down on the mud house and it was leaking like a sieve. Something caught my eye as we played. The shadow was moving down the wall in a slithering fashion. My heart stood still. Together, we stared at a snake that was sliding down the wall in an effort, perhaps, to get out of the rain. Without thinking, I ran to get my handy machete that we kept for such occasions as this. Knowing that he could not strike while coming down the wall, I cut him in half. He fell at my feet. Badly shaken, I had no desire to play more games that evening. Realizing that the rain showed no sign of letting up, we got up from the table and began putting buckets around the house to take care of the leaks.

Gene mentioned that he had not closed up the chicken house and that task should be done before some snakes got in to kill the chickens. The wind howled and whistled through the many palm trees that surrounded the mud house. I had real visions of several of them falling on the house, but I did not realize how God had created palm trees. They were made to survive the storms. As Gene stepped out into the blowing rain, the thought of being alone with the baby terrified me. Knowing that he would be wet and chilled when he returned, I thought of heating some water for a big cup of steaming tea. Cautiously, I opened the roughly made back screen door that led to an outside lean-to. It had some makeshift cupboards, a wood burning stove and a small kerosene pump stove made by the Chinese. There was only an open doorway and window openings covered by village made bamboo shutters. These were to keep the torrential rains from pouring in.

I busied myself trying to get the kerosene stove lit properly. Getting a nice hot, blue flame that would boil water wasn't easy. The breeze coming in from the open doorway was blowing away at the flame. Boiling water that night would test my patience; I could see that peering out into the pitch darkness gave me an uneasy feeling. There was nothing to protect me with that open doorway. I was constantly comforted with the thought that Gene would soon return. Actually, he wasn't that far from the house. As the water heated, I thought it best to go inside and wait in a far safer area. Turning to enter the house, I was confronted with a six to seven foot black cobra. I gasped in horror as I peered into the eyes of a serpent that was looking for a dry place to hide from the rain. He was blocking the only exit in or out of the lean-to kitchen. Knowing that time was short, I began to scream for my husband to come. Surely he would hear me and come running to save me from this venomous snake. The moments ticked by like an eternity. I screamed louder.

Outside, the wind blew harder and more intense. It was one of those tropical storms that show anger and fury. It was deafening! I knew in that instant that there was no help on the way for me. He could not hear and I was screaming in vain. Slowly, I backed into the corner. The snake rose up some eighteen inches in a striking position. Death was staring back at me. I had read what cobra venom did to its victims and the very thought of dying like that filled me with anger and an intense fear at the same time. Standing paralyzed to the spot, I looked intensely into his eyes and waited for his next move. The cobra arched to strike. Then, I felt the Presence of God. With strength now gone, I whispered the name of Jesus. My lips fell silent as I cried out to Him, "Oh Jesus, help me!"

I was in a capsule of silence. In an instant, the head of the black cobra hit the dirt very close to my feet. God had struck it down. A paralyzing sensation came over me as I watched the serpent turn in front of me. He returned to exit in a downpour of rain. The snake was surely seeking a dry place to hide when he first came in, but God had sent him again into the darkness, mud and rain. I huddled yet in the corner, crying, trembling and exhausted. My husband found me there and rushed to comfort me. In that moment, God showed me that my husband wouldn't always be with me. My lesson was a vivid one, one not to be forgotten.

The enormous region of the Likouala, a vast uncharted area, was home to thousands of people who had never heard about the saving Grace of God. My husband needed to move out with the Bible school students into every area of this territory and evangelize the people. He would often be gone during the vacation times when Bible school wasn't in session. Would I keep him from going because of fear?

Being alone with the children, I had to trust in the One who could keep me in every circumstance. I was to put that great lesson to the test many times throughout the years. Through government strife, through long lonely nights, God would keep me and the children in the hollow of His hand. That night, we offered up praises and adoration to the Lord for His safekeeping. I had faced the enemy and God was triumphant.

It didn't mean that I never had fear again, but I was better able to turn to God and seek His protection and claim His help. For He has said in Psalms 27:1, "The Lord is my light and my salvation; whom shall I fear? The Lord is the strength of my life; of whom shall I be afraid?

OH, THOSE CRAWLING CREATURES

It never occurred to me, in the beginning, that we would not be the only ones inhabiting the big, mud house. It was logical to believe that there might be a few crawling insects in the bamboo roof, but as long as they remained in their proper place, I had no plans to dislodge them. Oh, was I ever mistaken! The first tropical storm set my thinking straight. Only then did I realize that I would have to make room for some very unsavory visitors that were either wanted or unwanted. In my case, they were, in most part, unwanted.

French people from the Colonial Administration gave us a food magazine that really captured my attention. We could order many delicious items from France and the food would come by one kilo boxes. If the weather was good, the packets came up by riverboat from six hundred miles to the south of us in Brazzaville. If the weather was bad, like in rainy season, French military planes flew over the grassy airstrip and parachuted the packets to the ground. That was a thrilling event to break up our isolated life. It also gave us something different from the daily fare of rice, fish, spinach and the morning oatmeal.

I had found a wonderful recipe that called for some apricot nectar, so I ordered two small cans in an effort to make a very special cake for my husband. He had a sweet tooth and something so delicious and regal as that cake would set the stage for a somewhat time of celebration. All the extra calories didn't matter in those days as we needed them just to keep up our very thin bodies. In the lean-to kitchen, I busied myself by carefully sifting the flour over and over. This was to make sure that most of the little flour bugs could no longer be seen by the naked eye. I have to be candidly honest though that there were times when even repeated flour sifting did not rid it of those ever present little varmints. Because of the heat and humidity of the tropic, they made their abode in almost anything that was not sealed in Tupperware. African cuisine was a challenge to the missionary cook and without doubt, not one of us ever won in any measurable way. The bugs were the victors. Had I ever entertained such a life while living in America? I think not. Even the poorest cook in our country would never have presented her family with creamed tuna on toast points that also included bitty, bitty bugs.

Most of the time, we had no choice so it became my motto that what you can't see won't hurt you. To prove my point, we all survived the rigors of that life. However, I was creating a work of art and with some expensive nectar, and eggs that were saved from gifts that were given to us by the village women, there was nothing that would stop me from my labor of love. As the aroma wafted through the morning air, I was proud of myself for being able to overcome so many problems, including the opening and closing of the wood stove. The latter was done to keep the cake from rising too high on the side of the hot wood box. Perfecting this would be a real talent. Yes, the day was perfect.

Looking outside the lean-to kitchen, I noticed that the clouds were gathering and the sky seemed to have a menacing look about it. The gentle breeze was turning into a hefty wind as it came across the open Ubangui River. The many palm trees around the mud house were swaying back and forth in unison. A cake on a day such as this would prove to be an enjoyable blessing, or so I thought. My husband came home before the clouds opened up their windows to torrential rains. I was happy that I was able to get the cake iced with fluffy, seven minute icing before the downpour. The cake was carefully set on top of the large kerosene refrigerator to await the dessert hour. Puddles were beginning to form on the dirt floor so the cake was forgotten as we scurried around the mud house to put buckets in various places. The bamboo roof leaked badly, but didn't they all? We were learning that this was a small price to pay, as long as the rain did not come down on the bed or on the office desk. Failing to have many buckets on hand resulted in holes in the dirt floor. These could be quite an inconvenience if one was not watching where one was walking. One twisted ankle was a good reminder for the next time.

Evening was coming on. The rain was subsiding a little and we left the buckets to remain in their various places for the rest of the night. It was time for supper and I had a wonderful surprise. We ate our soup made from Nile perch fish head, and then it was time to bring out the prize. I was so proud of myself. Walking to the kerosene refrigerator, I brought down my beautiful cake. I sent out a loud cry of distress. My husband came running. He looked at me and then at my apricot nectar cake. Within the fluffy piles of soft, yellow icing, were dead spiders, pieces of dirty bamboo and other small, dead items that looked like ants or pieces of partially eaten lizards. As the tears coursed down my face, Gene put his arms around me and tried, without success, to comfort me. He assured me that he would scoop out all the unwanted dead, dried, unsavory creatures and there would still be enough fluffy icing to grace the elegant nectar cake. The very sight and thoughts of where they came from was enough to stem my desires for even the smallest slice. The day and evening had been completely ruined and I knew in the depths of my heart that there could be no spiritual lessons to be learned from this day's events. I was so wrong! Other experiences would pale besides this particular happening and would fade away in memory as God continued to teach us in the school of life. It would take time to learn to live and survive in this jungle land but how could we be really happy and share God's Word with others who were waiting along the many rivers back in the deep forest. How patient our Lord needed to be with us. So often we grieved Him because of our slowness to accept His teaching methods. When a person answers the call to missions, he or she must also accept the ways in which He desires to prepare us for our particular ministry. We were going to be His life long students.

Days turned into weeks and the cake episode was forgotten, except for one brief thought. I decided, in the privacy of my heart, that I would never again waste precious items on another "elegant nectar cake."

From the beginning, I never had a fear of mice or the large, black and orange lizards with long tails, but I did not like to share my mud house with the fat jungle rats that sometimes sought entrance into our humble home. They could be destructive and we knew that their razor like teeth could be like a grinding mill. All dried food stuffs had to be kept in steel drums in an effort to keep the food dry and away from hungry rats. The village people enjoyed eating them because they had a lot of meat on their bones. The jungle rat was unlike the house rats. Those from the jungle lived on herbs and seemed more like a groundhog. Gene did learn to eat them when he was traveling with the Bible school students back along the interior rivers. He said that they were quite tasty when garlic and hot peppers were added to the sauce. I never was brave enough to try this so called delicacy. It appeared to me that the village people had learned how to turn all these villains into succulent dishes for their evening meals. Perhaps later, I would be able to share this "savory" dish, but it would be sometime in the future, and maybe never.

In the private moments of my fertile mind, I thought about the numerous snakes that the workmen were killing as they cut the ever growing grass around the mud house. They used machetes and sickles to hack away at the tough grass. There were no lawn movers in the beginning years. Often, a cry would go up from the workmen as they sighted a snake. They yelled, "Nyoka." At the sound of this word, everyone converged on the area with a good long pole to pursue the unwelcome visitor. Although we had screen doors in the mud house, the dirt under them would often give way due to the heavy rains that would carry away the dirt under the door and this allowed snakes an easy way in. With our busy schedule of learning the language and helping with the Lingala literacy classes, some items of importance fell by the wayside, such as making sure that the holes were filled up.

The seriousness of this was brought home to us one day when our little daughter, Joy, was playing outside in the grass. Both of us were at a desk in the office typing lessons and letters. From time to time, we looked out to make sure that she was okay. Suddenly, Gene got up and stated that the ducks were acting funny. Usually, when they make strange noises and walk off to one side, there is danger close by. Studying the grass, he saw movement. Very slowly and deliberately, a green mamba rose up and observed the surroundings. In a second, I ran to scoop up little Joy and Gene yelled for the workmen to come with their machetes. With all the men converging on one spot, he yelled for them not to strike out with a stick because green mambas can turn backward in a split second and strike the victim. Not listening to the instruction, one young man took his long stick and struck out at the snake. The mamba turned backward with all its force and almost struck the man named Bandamba. The group of men turned their forces to the serpent and killed it without hesitation. Later that afternoon, we left the house for a very short period of time. As we cleared the open office door, a black cobra slithered in and wrapped itself around the treadle sewing machine wheel. Getting him to leave so that we could enter was a difficult task. He had claimed a home and wasn't about to give it up. Another war was waged before we were able to enter the house in safety. We had come into a hostile area and dealing with serpents would become a way of life, one that would test our faith over and over. The mud house had become a battle ground.

One night around midnight, I felt the need to get up and make a little trip to the outhouse, a short distance

A dead green mamba snake

from the mud house. Almost two years had passed and I really felt quite secure in our surroundings despite all the encounters that we had had with snakes. The night lantern turned low, but I was able to see sufficiently to pull the mosquito netting out from the mattress and tuck it under again. Long heavy strings held the mosquito netting high where it was tied to the rafters of the bamboo roof. I sat for a minute and watched the shows that were cast on the white washed walls.

Our daughter, Joy was asleep in her crudely made baby bed. I could hear the soft coos as she slept. My shoes were on the mat at the side of the bed where I was getting out. As I pushed back the net and slipped my feet into the sandals, I felt a very sharp pain to the ankle. I cried out in pain and awakened my husband who had been sleeping soundly. Explaining to him what had happened, he got up and looked around but he didn't see much in the dimly lit room. I proceeded to go outside along the narrow pathway. My flashlight picked out a crocodile that was lying nearby. I frightened him and he slid off the

The fangs of the green mamba

bank and into the dark waters. Returning to the house, I experienced a greater intensity of pain. Gene thought that I had been bitten by some of the many ants that invaded the house on a regular basis. I didn't want to act like a baby, so I crawled back into bed and the security of the mosquito net.

Morning came quickly and we both knew that something was very wrong. My leg was swollen and a red line had streaked up as far as the hip. Nausea and fever overtook me. Gene got on his pedal bike and went to the small hospital where there was a resident French doctor. A Vietnamese doctor was on staff, a very kind and gentle man who was married to a French lady. They had befriended us on many occasions and we felt sure that he would come if we called him. He did return along the jungle path until he came to our mud house. He checked me over and his diagnosis wasn't what we wanted to hear. His prognosis was that I had been bitten by a poisonous snake and showed us the bite marks that he felt were made by a cobra. He measured the distance of the fang marks and the depth. We were not immediately afraid because we felt certain that the hospital would surely keep sufficient snake serum on hand, being that we were in an environment of this nature. When we asked him for the serum to stem the deadly poison, he shook his head and simply stated that there was none at all. The doctor left saying that he would order some by radio telephone, but that it wasn't likely that any would arrive until the next boat came in. That could be a week away.

After hearing of the numbers of Congolese who had died of snake bites, we knew that it was a matter of hours before my life would be over and that of our unborn son who was to arrive in three months.

As my husband sat by my side on the bed, we remembered so vividly how God had placed His hands on us for foreign service. We had heard His call and responded. Was it all to end like this? As his tears fell on my face, he cast his body across mine and wailed before the Throne of Grace. He was quoting to God our life verse from Proverbs 3:5,6,7,8 "Trust in the Lord with all thine heart; and lean not unto thine own understanding. In all thy ways acknowledge Him, and He shall direct thy paths. Be not wise in thine own eyes: fear the Lord, and depart from evil. It shall be health to thy navel, and marrow to thy bones." He waited by the edge of the bed for hours. It seemed like an eternity passed. The long day turned into another night and I was still alive. Instead of getting worse, I felt strength coming back into my body. The red poison line had stopped at the hip when prayer began.

Alone at a jungle station and away from good medical treatment, God had met us at the Throne of Grace, just as much as He had met Jacob the night that he slept under the open Heaven and an angel came to struggle with him. That night, Jacob came to a milestone in his life and named the place where he had met God. We, too, saw our impossible situation and claimed the power of a great and mighty God, the One Who had called us to this forsaken area. We could not and would not survive to become old if His Presence was not with us. Was it possible that we could rise to the challenge of life in this land of wild animals, serpents and disease? We had many questions after this incident but the answers would be slow in coming. We were left with no doubt that He would not allow us to confront more situations that we could bear. At a crucial juncture in the road, our Heavenly Father was there to carry us in His arms of love and protection.

LEOPARDS LURKING IN THE SHADOWS

The new day was just breaking over the distant horizon when Gene and a Bible school student left the mission station to evangelize every village deep in the jungles and beyond the swamps of the Congo Basin. I packed filtered water and a good lunch. No seven to eleven stores were available where they were going. If you didn't have what you needed when you got to your destination, it was much too late to think about it. They put bicycle supply parts in a box and tied that to the pedal bike. The morning heat

Gene on a bicycle

and humidity were already settling in. The day would prove to be stifling and hard to endure. Their bodies would have to stand up under difficult climactic conditions. It made us wonder about Jesus and his disciples as they walked over hot, dusty roads and sometimes bumped along on the hard and uncomfortable back of a donkey. Preaching the Gospel was done by men who were not afraid to hazard their lives for Christ. Looking for luxury accommodations was not a part of their thinking.

As Gene left, he kissed me and said that he would, hopefully, be back at dark, which would be around six p.m. They had miles to go and much work was before them. Most of the people in the dense forest had never heard the Way of Salvation. Because of this, the fellows felt an awesome responsible that they might hear. These trips were taken very seriously. In the years to follow, we would want to build churches among the new Christians who were reached from these periodic bike visits into these vast and hidden areas of the forbidden jungle.

The forest was

Sandy on a bicycle

wild and full of many dangers on every hand. There were elephants tearing down areas of the forest. Wild buffalo roamed the high grass on the plains near the jungles and leopards, chimps, monkeys, gorillas and many species of dangerous snakes inhabited the unknown behind the jungle wall. As I watched them disappear down the narrow path, my heart immediately became ill at ease. So many things could go wrong and there was no means of communicating with the home base. I thought to myself that missionary women had to be self trained to be brave and vigilant at the same time.

The day was before me and there was much work to do to keep me occupied. Locking the office door behind me, I sat at the typewriter. Behind me were two small children one year apart. How I ever managed to get anything done with all their noise is beyond me. The day wore on and I was nervous because night was approaching and the fellows had not arrived home. Despite the warnings in my heart, I put our young son on the back of the bike, in a wicker seat, and pedaled away from the

Native woman packing a heavy load

mission compound. I really hadn't intended to go too far, but just far enough to meet the two bikers.

As I went along, the path became narrower and the elephant grass was too tall. Something was telling me that maybe I should turn back. But, I argued with myself that there was no immediate danger. Riding more slowly now, I met up with many village women who were returning to the village from the forest. They had gone out to their gardens before dawn and stayed all day to dig and plant. From time to time, the husbands went with the women to cut down the tall trees so that the sun could shine through. Later, when the trees dried, precious firewood would be gathered. The gardens of eating and cooking bananas were a major source of

Women with heavy loads are common

money for the family. The cooking bananas were pounded and made into loaves for sale in front of the house or at the market place. Manioc was a staple also that was prepared much like the cooking bananas. Pineapples, white sweet potatoes and field corn were added to this array of foods.

The women carried unbelievable weights that would stagger even a husky man. Not only would their back baskets be filled with food, but on the top of them, dry firewood was carefully placed above and around everything. Wood was always needed for cooking and with the trees being cut down close to the village; they had to go farther and farther away to find more. It was not unusual to see a baby in a sling being carried in front of the women. I don't think that I ever observed these hard working women without thinking of God's Word that offered a new hope for the weary. "Come unto me, all ye that labor and are heavy laden and I will give you rest. Take my yoke upon you and learn of me; for I am meek and lowly in heart: and ye shall find rest unto your souls. For my yoke is easy, and my burden is light" (Matthew 11:28-30).

The day would come when many of them would know and understand the meaning of this wonderful promise from God. Even though the loads were the kinds that donkey's would carry, they would still raise their bent body and take a moment to look up and greet me with a smile and say, "Mbote!" This meant, "Hello." Others would call out and ask, "Ojali kokenda wapi Madame?" (Where are you going Madame?) When I answered that I was going down the jungle trail to meet the pastor, they would call back and say that they had not seen him and that it would be wise to turn around and go home before dark. Passing the last large group of women, I observed, more closely, my surroundings. The monkeys were swinging from the tree branches and chattering loudly to one another. Evidently an announcement was being made that a stranger was in their midst. The chirping birds flew around excitedly as they sought to find a secure resting place for the long night. The dense foliage afforded them that unique comfort and protection. The farther I went; the jungle became extremely hot and steamy. Aside from the chirping birds and the chattering monkeys, there was an awful stillness. That strange feeling of being totally alone came over me. I stopped for a moment and called Gene's name. No sound was heard, no response.

Arriving at the crest of a hill, I looked down the long, weedy path that lead to the dreaded swamps filled with snakes of every description. It was known also as a haven for the Falciparum mosquitoes that carried malaria. The stench of the swamp gases was almost overwhelming.

Sizing up the situation and the path downhill, I observed that the overhanging vines in the trees cut out much of the light. Night was coming quickly. I peered through the maze of twisted trees. Trying to be brave, my mind was made up to go down the hill and stop by a burned out tree stump that seemed to be hunkering down in the tall grass. I looked at it a long time before leaving my present position.

Actually, we had been that way before but, I had never noticed the burned out stump. It must have been cut and burned since the last time we had been there. In the stillness, I was painfully aware that my heart was pounding in my chest. It was so loud that my ears throbbed and my chest hurt. Still being brave, I reasoned and assured myself that I would stop the bike and turn around at the tree stump. The long elephant grass and biting weeds were reaching out to my sweaty legs causing them to itch and hurt. They had a terrible abrasive effect that annoyed me to no end. Carefully, I inched forward and approached the stump. I stopped abruptly. Darkness was slowly engulfing me. I was limp with fear. Turning the bike around in the tangle of weeds was extremely difficult. Vines had woven themselves around the underbrush to form a unique haven for jungle rats. It was also a perfect home for snakes waiting for an evening meal. That thought brought a wave of chills and sweat. What else was here?

Stopping suddenly, I heard a strange panting sound. My feet were cemented to the spot. A black panther was hardly visible at first but her piercing, bloodshot eyes met mine. Fear had me in its grip so badly that I could not scream or utter a noise. This mother panther with a little one was a recipe for disaster. A poorly thought out plan could have led to a mauling for me and my son. I don't recall if I prayed, but I do know that God was with me in my foolishness. He must have pinched the panther because she leaped high above the tall grass, with a loud screech, and then she disappeared into the dense, dark forest. The danger was gone.

There were other hurdles to surmount. How could I possibly get up the hill that I had just come down? With the fear and excitement, I had forgotten my son who was still sitting in the basket seat behind me. He had remained quiet during this entire incident. One fact remained. It was not possible to pedal up the hill. My rubbery legs were too heavy to perform the simple task of pedaling. My breath was coming in quick pants. Help was needed, but there was none. Ever so slowly, I began pushing the bike uphill. Why had I done such a foolish thing? Questions were tumbling around in my mind. Upon arriving at the Mission, the Congolese berated me for going off alone. Indeed, it was a foolish act, but a valuable lesson had been learned.

Little by little, incidents such as this one taught me about life in this jungle land. Later that night, Gene and Pierre pedaled into the Impfondo mission station. Being a missionary was exciting but it was also dangerous. Hazards seemed to await us at every turn of the river and at the end of every endless trail. The call of God was a call to self-denial and a willingness to forge ahead at any cost.

The men were bone weary from the long and difficult trip. The good part was that they reached so many forest people who heard Jesus calling them unto life everlasting. Some believed and many still doubted. It would take years and much effort to do a lasting work. The men would need to go many more times to teach God's Word before the people would cast off their fetishes and witchcraft and embrace God's plan for them. Gene and Pierre reviewed their whole trip. They had had flat tires that slowed them up considerably. Elephant excrement was seen on the trail. The large animals had recently been there.

On paths crossing theirs, the pungent smell of leopard urine was noted. Without doubt, they were lurking nearby. Joshua must have felt much like us missionaries when he took over Moses' task after Moses died. God spoke to Joshua and gave him many promises. He said, "As I was with Moses, so I will be with thee; I will not fail thee, nor forsake thee. Be strong and of good courage: Only be thou strong and very courageous . . . This Book of the Law shall not depart out of thy mouth; but thou shalt meditate therein day and night, that thou mayest observe to do according to all that is written therein: for then thou shalt make thy way prosperous, and then thou shalt have good success" (Joshua 1:5b, 6a, 7a, v.8).

God heard the cries of the lost and it was His plan to bring them the Bread of Life. It was a story of triumph over dangers and hardships. We would, like soldiers, go and face the enemy of our souls. The pelting rains, the boiling hot sun and the never ending bites from tropical flies and mosquitoes often put a damper on our spirits, but these were mere momentary obstacles to challenge our resolve for Christ. Hadn't Jesus passed this way before? Being on a mission for Him, we felt convinced that our Heavenly Father would keep watch over us and never allow the enemy to overcome us in any way. That part had been settled years before when we dedicated our lives to do service for Him in this difficult area of the world. It was always comforting to feel His Presence during dangerous journeys into the jungles and along the waterways. We had both read many missionary stories of those who had served in places such as ours, but to experience this strange way of life was very different. The secret was being in the perfect will of God.

GEORGE,
THE BOY WOODCUTTER

Each day after school, young George hurried up the dirt road past a section of jungle and arrived at our mud house. He would take the large pieces of wood that we bought from the woodcutters and begin the tedious and often difficult task of cutting and chopping it into small pieces. Using the ax was not an easy job for a lad such as George, but he never complained. To make the time go faster, he sang the songs from his family and tribe. He did not know it, but he was helping us to cope with this major change in our lives. At every turn, we needed help in understanding the people and their ways and young George was there to give us words of wisdom about the culture and educate us on the African mindset. In this manner, he proved to be much more valuable than just a woodcutter, although he was never aware of this.

While living in our mud house, we were busy making plans to build a permanent brick home. This was no small feat. Clay from termite hills was put into two brick molds and then sent to a drying shed. After thousands of bricks had been made and dried, they were put into an enormous kiln. After burning them for six days and nights, they turned into beautiful red fire brick. Although the house looked rather modern for jungle standards, it was unique in its own way because there were no ceilings for eighteen years. This allowed the mosquitoes to take residence with us, too. The wood stove was brought over from the outside kitchen of the mud house and put into a brick outside kitchen. This helped to keep the intense heat away from the house itself as temperatures and humidity were overwhelming to us.

The lad, George, had grown into a handsome young man. He had been like a member of our family for a long time and hardly anyone noticed that his boyhood years had come to a close. In the beginning, it seemed that he would always be there to work for us and give us counsel in our new African life.

One day, George came to work on a Saturday rather early. It wasn't his habit to do this and we knew that something was bothering him a great deal. He waited until we had eaten our breakfast and then he asked to talk to us. Quietly, he sat down and hesitated before he began to speak. He related to us how he had first come to work for us and how much he loved being not only a part of the family, but also a part of the church were he had come to know Christ as his personal Savior. He had talked with his

A long paddle boat

sister, Emile, about his future and she suggested that he return to their country of the Central African Republic. You see, it was time for him to think of looking for a wife among the young women of his tribe, and then establish a home of his own.

We were sad to think of him leaving but having learned so much about the culture of the people, we knew that it was time for him to make his way in the world. A

party was planned to celebrate his time among us and his plans for departure. We all kissed him goodbye and watched as he waved his final farewell from the old paddle boat that pulled away

Brick kilns for firing bricks

from the shore and started its slow journey up the Ubangui River to Bangui, Central Africa, some 250 miles to the north of Impfondo. It seemed likely that we would never meet him again and the thought saddened our hearts.

In 1967, after the premature birth of our third child, it became an impossible task for me to continue teaching the two oldest children, Joy and Steven. They had finished fifth grade and the time had come to send them away to Mission school. No one will ever know, except other missionaries, the heartrending decisions that are made when having to send children away to another country for schooling. We discussed it at great length. We cried about it. We prayed. The children needed to be with their peers and learn more about life among other American children. As it was, they preferred to speak the native language more than their own. Our children's mannerisms were Congolese and culturally, they were being integrated into the Congolese culture and not their own. As parents, we tried in vain to change what they were becoming but it was an impossible task, due to the fact that they were actually out of their very own country.

A Mission school in the Central African Republic was contacted and they agreed to take our two children. Because there was an American Embassy in the capital city of Bangui in that country, with which the Americans enjoyed good relations, we were able to go in and out without having to get visas, which is often a costly, lengthy and time consuming process. A few years passed by and

Press for molding bricks

the President of the Central African Republic made himself an Emperor. With diamonds, gold and much ivory in his country, he was a very wealthy man, and also quite sadistic and cruel. Some American journalists were given an audience to see him. Upon entering the throne room, they reached out their hands to shake his hand. They were, in fact, supposed to kiss his hand or thumb. With the large ring on his hand, he struck one of the journalists in the face and broke his nose. They were both thrown in prison and it took a number of months for the American Embassy to secure their release.

The Emperor was now becoming irate with the Americans because they looked on his activities in a questionable manner. He was also making good friends with Kadafi, the ruler of Libya whose country was north of the Central Africa Republic (CAR). With relations becoming more strained between America and CAR, the Emperor suddenly made it mandatory for Americans to get a visa when entering the country. Likewise, the U.S. retaliated and made it necessary for the people of CAR to get a visa when entering our country.

At the beginning of December, it was time to go north to pick up our children when they came down by truck from the mission school in Kaga Bandoro, Central Africa. Because our last daughter was still very small and fragile, Gene went alone on the long trip to the Central African Republic.

Arriving at the beach in Bangui, the capital, he tied up the speedboat where the French kept their boats. This was the way he had always done it. This day would be quite different. From behind him, a beach guard approached and asked for his Passport. After the man looked through the Passport, he noticed that there was no visa. He asked for an explanation. Gene went on to explain that he didn't need a visa. He had come up many times and since he would be in and out in twenty-four hours, it was not required. It was becoming very evident that the young border guard had not been around very long and was not aware of former regulations. He only knew now that there was no visa stamped in that Passport. When Gene tried to explain again, the guard yelled at him to shut up and start walking down the red dusty road. Children along the way were amused and giggled as they watched the white man with a gun to his back.

The guard was muttering words under his breath that indeed a spy had invaded their land and he would have to be taken care of. Gene had no knowledge of where he was being taken. He was overwhelmed by fear in his heart and for the gun in his ribs. Glancing ahead, he observed a dirty government building that had not been painted in a very long time. The military man's strong arm pushed him toward the rickety old door. They entered together and the guard promptly left him alone. Sitting down on a well-worn chair in the waiting room, Gene bowed his head to pray for help. Pictures of two American journalists raced across his mental screen. We had heard, by radio, that these men had been arrested, beaten and thrown into an unbelievably filthy prison cell. What had they done to deserve all this? They had failed to greet the self-imposed Emperor in a proper way. They reached out to shake hands with him instead of bowing and kissing his ring finger. Gene knew that the American Ambassador had the men freed only after long government meetings. If he were to be thrown in this prison, no one would know of his fate or his whereabouts. The situation was critical and it was a time when only God could intervene and set him free.

Being in a foreign country can be a frightening experience when problems of this magnitude arise. He had no idea how long he sat with bowed head praying to God to intervene. With his head still lowered, he opened his eyes. Between his own two separated legs, he saw the boots of a military man. There was total silence as each stared at the other. The young man smiled and said in our language of Lingala, "Pastor Thomas is that really you?"

There was a long pause as Gene struggled to remember this tall young man. The people of the Central African Republic spoke Sango. They didn't know our language. How then was this man speaking in Lingala? Gene again studied his face and finally spoke. "Is that you George? Is that really you? What are you doing here?"

"I asked you first, so tell me what has happened." George replied.

Knowing that no one could understand them in the office, Gene spoke to George in Lingala rather than in French so that no one knew what they were discussing. French was used by foreigners in a government office. Gene quickly recounted to George what had happened at the beach with the young border guard who just then was coming out the main office. George was alarmed that a gun had been put to Gene's back.

Having heard the whole story, George asked Gene to follow him into the office of the director. Gene was extremely hesitant to follow him because he noticed that George was only a private. Nevertheless, George insisted that he follow and they opened the door to the office of the Minister of the Interior. As Gene stood before the minister, it was evident that the man knew who George was and he was treated with a great deal of respect. George began telling the minister about his life with Pastor Thomas who had raised him as a son. Pastor Thomas had taught him how to do a little boxing and that he and his wife had given him a lot of love and care during his formative years. There were times during the stories that Gene felt like he had a few wings on as the stories became somewhat exaggerated. The stories had made a powerful impact on the man behind the desk. The door opened and a secretary walked in with some passports.

"Is this your passport?" he questioned.

Gene assured him that it was. It was handed to him and he was told that he was free to go. Outside the building, Gene was interested in finding out some vital information. What was George doing in that building that day? How was it that he just happened to come to that place just when he was greatly needed? What were his official duties? George laughed a little and said that it was his duty to pass by all the government offices every day to make sure that the men were on duty and carrying out their particular functions. Why had he come just then? He had no answer for that. They both knew he had been appointed by God to come and spare Gene of something that could have been very serious. His real job was being the personal bodyguard of the Emperor of the country. That job is only given to men of a President's own tribe and they have no decision as far as refusing the position. Once it is appointed, one must obey or it could mean death.

Later on when Gene arrived at the Mission for the night, he looked at his Passport. In it was a visa for life, something that no missionary can obtain. That Passport is still among our prized possessions to prove what God does for those who pray and place their trust in Him. This was ordained by God. God knew long ago that this little woodcutter named, George, would someday be used to spare one of His servants a painful experience and maybe even death. Never did we leave home or a foreign place without first offering ourselves up before the Throne of Grace. We prayed for mercy and help in time of need and urgency.

He has never failed us at any time, but has delivered us from oppressors and circumstances in which there was no way out. David must have felt that way in Psalm 18:1-4, 6, 46 as he sang a Psalm of deliverance to his God. He spoke words of this song in the day that the Lord delivered him from the hand of all his enemies.

"I will love thee, O Lord, my strength. The Lord is my rock, and my fortress, and my deliverer; my God, my strength, in whom I will trust; my buckler, and the horn of my salvation, and my high tower. I will call upon the Lord, who is worthy to be praised: so shall I be saved from my enemies. In my distress I called upon the Lord, and cried unto my God: he heard my voice out of his temple, and my cry came before him, even into his ears. The Lord liveth; and blessed be my Rock; and let the God of my salvation be exalted."

The lesson was well learned in that country. The little unknown man or woman that we befriended in some out of way place was often used in the ensuing years to give help in time of need. God knows our comings and our goings and He will use the woodcutter today to bring help to you tomorrow.

THE SLEEPING GIANT AWAKENS

The year was 1965 and Africa was like a pot of boiling water. Millions were restless and looking for an identity. Communism was waving its red flag toward the continent and for some reason, it seemed interesting. The years of colonization were fast coming to a close. Under the French colonial masters, Africa had been sleeping. It was dulled into a false security that the future would bring them a sense of status and betterment. But, the colonialists had not planned on making their colonies

Communist military in the Congo

independent and when they were forced to hand over the reigns of power, most of Africa was unprepared to rule themselves. Immediately, the power struggles began.

Many tribal groups raised their voices in defiance to take over smaller tribes. It wasn't a matter of what was right for the country that they all lived in but what was right for the more educated and powerful. A terrible civil war was waged across river in the former Belgian Congo. Tens of thousands of people were killed and many more had to flee for their lives. We, living in the Congo, colonized by France, were watching as the French were being replaced, in part, by the Russians, Chinese and other eastern block countries. Returning from furlough, we were shocked to see the heavy military presence. The quiet and peaceful city took on an appearance of war. Large groups of military men with machine guns were seen on the tops of buildings. We walked down the plane steps and walked across the tarmac between long lines of soldiers with submachine guns pointed at us. Even at night, we could hear small arms fire and there was an uneasy feeling among all of us missionaries. The country had shaken off their former colonial master and replaced that master for another, one much harsher and one that would prove very deadly. We checked in at the American Embassy and talked at length with the American Ambassador. He was alarmed that we had returned at such a time and suggested that we book passage to return to the United States. We were alarmed at his words.

We had two children and did not want to place their lives in any kind of jeopardy, but neither did we want to return to the United States. We had received a long term visa and felt that God did not want us to run away. We assured him that we would pray about the situation and return to discuss the subject again. As we rode through the city, we were being stopped at every major road to present our passports. Military were everywhere and we sensed that we were about to become a part of some catastrophic event.

A second visit to the Ambassador convinced us that we should buy supplies and book passage on a riverboat going north. We hurried, made out a long food list of canned goods and other basic needs that would keep us for a few months. We then had these supplies sent to the port of Brazzaville. The Swedish missionaries took us very early one morning to the boat. It was a good feeling to be away from the crowds of restless people and the military that seemed eager to use the guns strapped to their shoulders.

It seemed like an eternity before the boat whistle sounded and we finally inched our way out to the channel of the great Congo River. We settled down in our first class cabin and planned on enjoying our nine day trip up river to our station at Impfondo on the Ubangui River. The French boat captain and his wife had been replaced by a Congolese captain. We knew him personally, as well as many of his crew members. They were people from our area of Impfondo and this was a very comforting feeling. Our two children, Joy and Steven, played with the captain's children and they had a wonderful time as they tried once again to remember the Lingala language. The children felt that they had forgotten it all but after several hours, we heard them speaking Lingala as if they had never left the Congo. They were amazed that it all came back so quickly.

At mealtime, we met a man named Monga. He had a body built like many of our American football players. He had massive shoulders and was very tall and handsome. He was going to Impfondo also and was overjoyed that we knew almost everyone in his family. Some of them had come to the Lord under our ministry and we were able to talk at length about our knowledge of his people. Mr. Monga had been appointed the director of schools and besides visiting with his family members, he wanted to check on the condition of the school system in the Impfondo area and the whole region of the Likouala. Talk turned to politics and we shared with him our fears of what was going on in the capital city. He opened up his heart and told us that the government had called him back from France where he had been working and living with his French wife and their children. He secretly shared that the Congo was not ready to embrace something as tyrannical as Communism and he knew that the people would be brought into a slavery that they had never known before.

They had lived under a stern colonial French power but they did have roads, lovely schools, scholarships for advanced University training for the brightest students and they had hospitals and control of the tropical diseases. Medicine and care were free. The people seemed to have what they need and more, except that they had no control over their own country.

The sleeping giant was now moving and ready to take on a power more deadly than anyone had ever seen or experienced before. Instead of peace and prosperity, war and bloodshed would be the rally cry. Peace would never again reign in the Congo. War would always be that unwanted guest. Colonial powers had not foreseen this day. Mr. Monga, the passenger friend, talked with us long into the night. We felt glad that God had brought him into our lives.

Very early on the fourth day, about four a.m. in the morning, we were awakened by the boat moving slowly toward land. People were shouting loudly. At daylight, we peered out from our third deck and watched the dugout canoes as they tied up to the riverboat. Canoes were loaded with bananas, plantains, sweet potatoes, greens, fish, dried meat and pineapples. It was wonderful to look down and watch all the villagers as they bartered with passengers on the barges. We were now back home and it was a good feeling.

Suddenly, there was the sound of gunfire and we went to look down from the front of the third story of the boat. Military had come aboard and they were pushing the passengers and treating them badly as they yelled at them to present their identification papers. This meant that everyone on the boat would have to present papers to the military authorities. Gene looked down at the seriousness of the situation and came to a conclusion. We had heard from the boat captain, the night before, that the American Embassy personnel had closed the Embassy and all had fled the country. Since there were no other Americans in the South, it was evident that we were among the last remaining expatriates in the country. We knew the military could be hostile to us because of the departure of Embassy personnel. Gene asked that I and the children remain in the small cabin. I entered the cabin and locked the door behind me. I peered down on the barge where people were milling about. As soon as Gene appeared, he was set apart from the crowd. We were the only white people on the boat and the military quickly took note of this. He began showing our passports and I could readily tell that they were screaming at him. Hatred filled their eyes as they yelled out that he was an American. He tried in vain to tell them that he was a missionary but they were not interested in what he did, only who he was.

The air seemed electrified as all the young militants surrounded Gene. Each young man had a gun pointed toward him and in that moment, he felt that they were going to take his life. They accused him of being a spy so that they could stir up the feelings of the crowd of people that stood looking on. I stood before the cabin window totally terrified. An excuse was needed to pull the trigger and what better excuse could they have than to shoot a traitor or a spy against the country. Gene stood rigid and prayed in his heart. Without warning, a giant of a man stepped through the crowd and ripped the gun out of the hand of one of the militants.

He yelled, "What do you think that you are doing?"

The militant explained that the white man was a traitor and a spy and needed to be killed. He was also an American. The large man was Mr. Monga. This gentleman had once represented the Congo in International Competition and had received a silver medal as a javelin thrower. Almost everyone knew him. His picture was everywhere on walls and in publications. The youth of the Red Guard Movement looked up at him and asked his forgiveness for what they had intended to do. Mr. Monga took the passports from the hand of the militant who was looking at them and returned them to Gene. As he reached for the passport, he turned and looked up at the window of our cabin. My tears were running down the window. Gene hurried up the steps of the boat and I let him in the cabin. We wept together. God had intervened in a dramatic way. He had spared our lives that we might continue to serve Him.

Little could we know the awful things that lay ahead. Our lives would be threatened again and again and our names would be put on hit lists that we might be exterminated. We were soon to find out that our God is greater than the forces of Communism, greater than guns and greater than all the evil intentions of man.

In Bible times, there was a man called Hezekiah. Sennacherib, King of Assyria, invaded Judah. He laid siege to the fortified cities and desired to conquer them all for himself. But God wasn't for Sennacherib; he was with his servant, Hezekiah. At a time of vulnerability, when it seemed they would be overtaken, Hezekiah assembled his officers in the square of the city. He spoke words that have reverberated down through the ages of time, "Be strong and courageous, be not afraid nor dismayed for the king of Assyria, nor for all the multitude that is with him: for there be more with us than with him: With him is an arm of flesh; but with us is the Lord our God to help us, and to fight our battles" (II Chronicles 32:7, 8). The enemy would have devoured us, but God fought the battle and was victorious.

Three months after the time that God used this man to intervene for us, the government forces sent men to Mr. Monga's home in Brazzaville, the capital, and shot him five times in the head. As he lay dying in the arms of his uncle, he asked that his body be sent to his village to be buried near his family. As the riverboat approached Impfondo, local officials drove into the mission station with great haste. They asked for the use of our small 14-ft speedboat that had previously been given us when the U.S. Embassy left the Congo. The officials felt that it was necessary to go down below the village and pick up the body of Mr. Monga. Several thousand people were milling about the waterfront in a frenzied mood as they waited for the arrival of the riverboat.

Since the death of Mr. Monga, there was a great deal of unrest in the village and it was feared that a riot might break out. How ironic it was that the very man God used to intervene for Gene and save his life was now being carried, by Gene, to the banks of his family home. In the hour of greatest tragedy and fear, our Lord stands by His people to help them overcome the adverse circumstances of life. Fear is one of Satan's greatest tools.

If he can keep us in a state of fear, he will be able to

defeat us at the very time that God wants to use us the most. God was certainly shouting to us from the rooftops as we began a new term of service. He was saying loud and clear, "Fear thou not; for I am with thee: be not dismayed; for I am thy God: I will strengthen thee; yea, I will help thee; yea, I will uphold thee with the right hand of my righteousness" (Isaiah 41:10).

THE ULTIMATE SACRIFICE

It was about five o'clock in the evening when one of the station workmen came to the house and told us that there would be a sacrifice in the evening about sunset. We had read about sacrifices in missionary books and we wondered if it might be a human being. The workman explained that many years before, it was mostly Pygmies who were sacrificed to meet the demands of a village chief.

There were many villages along various waterways back in the deep jungle. Sometimes there were troubles between the villagers and various tribes. War would be declared and when the villagers passed by going to Impfondo, the main Post in the area, some of them would be killed by bows with poison arrows. This led to much hate and animosity among the people. They were afraid to travel between villages lest they be killed. Sometimes, they took hostages instead of killing their enemies. The chief of that village would then declare that he would release the hostage if a ransom was paid or a human sacrifice was given. Since the Pygmies were slaves, they had no choice in the affair but to be killed to meet the demands of the villagers who held the hostage or hostages.

At sunset, the Pygmy would be prepared for the ultimate sacrifice. Blood had to be shed. He was given palm or honey wine to make him very drunk and he would be asked to sing about his life and ancestors. Just before sunset, the machete to be used for the sacrifice would be sharpened until the metal shone. The old village chief, Makoko, recounted many stories of these events, also, and said that the Pygmies would often cry as they anticipated their life having to be given to free another. It was always a very sad occasion.

We wondered about this rite and asked ourselves if we should even be there. There would be much drinking beforehand and it was possible that this could lead to a crowd becoming frantic and out of control. We worked out a plan whereby we would go down to the center of the village on our bikes just before the setting of the sun at 6 p.m. The tall palms cast their shadows on the path as we hurried to the village. Instead of a Pygmy, they had chosen a goat for the sacrifice. He was tied to a stake and his neck was stretched out taut in preparation for the knife that would decapitate him. His feeble cries reminded us of what it must have been like in the Old Testament when a lamb was sacrificed, a symbol of Jesus Christ, Who would come someday and be the ultimate sacrifice, the LAMB OF GOD, Who died for the sins of the whole world.

The crowd of people was cheering. They became deathly silent. Every eye was on the villager who would cut the head off. Our camera was ready to flash the event. Our hearts were pounding as we stood behind the crowd but still close enough so that we could get a good picture. The shiny machete was raised. The man poised himself and took advantage of all the attention that was being given to him. Like lightning, the sharp knife came across the goat's neck and Gene pushed the camera button. He got the picture as the knife cut through the neck and the blood spurted on the crowd of onlookers. The head lay in a pool of blood while the muscles of the body twitched for a few seconds.

Seeing the flashing light of the camera gave the crowd the impression that there was a spirit present and they screamed, "He has power." They were referring to the man who had cut the head off with one slice of the machete.

A dog came to the center of the scene and began licking up the blood. Another picture was snapped and this time the people turned and saw us. Darkness had almost fallen but our presence was revealed. Seeing the anger in their eyes that we had come to observe a very private affair, they turned on us. We picked up our bikes that were nearby, mounted them and rushed off into the darkness. No one followed and we were relieved.

With so many drunk from hours of sipping their very potent homemade brew, it was not wise to stay on to discuss our desires of getting some good pictures. The results could have been very disastrous for us. Arriving at the house, we recounted what we had seen and the meaning of what we had done.

After many years of preaching the gospel, this practice was done away with. Only in the deep, deep jungles and away from law enforcement, there were repeated stories of human sacrifices.

In 1990, lawyers were sent up from the capital city to have a trial to try a number of people who had sacrificed people and ate their flesh. Eating human flesh was a sign of strength to overcome one's enemies. The emperor of the Central African Republic had killed his enemies and served the meat unknowingly to visiting African dignitaries. Pictures flashed around the world, some years ago, of the freezer lockers of Emperor Bokassa in the Central African Republic. He stated that he had overcome all his enemies by killing them and eating their flesh. It is a real sign of the unregenerate man when Jesus Christ is not allowed to reign the hearts of those whom God created.

As time went by, hundreds and then thousands came to a saving knowledge of Christ. The old things of this world had passed away because they were now new creatures.

In the book of I Samuel 15:22, Samuel spoke harshly to King Saul and grieved that he had made him king because of the condition of his heart. Samuel spoke these words to him, "Hath the Lord as great delight in burnt offerings and sacrifices, as in obeying the voice of the Lord? Behold, to obey is better than sacrifice, and to hearken than the fat of rams."

Those people ignored God, along with Saul, the king, and continued on in their sin, along with their leader, but the few who followed God found His blessings and protection. We, too, want to give God something other than our very lives. God is not interested in what we have materially, nor in our money. He is interested in us that we might give Him our heart.

When we, in obedience to God, went to the Congolese people, many thousands came out of the darkness unto the Light of salvation and followed Him unto life everlasting.

He is calling you today, not to make animal sacrifices, but to believe in the Ultimate Sacrifice, Jesus Christ Himself.

SAFE IN THE ARMS OF JESUS

Life at the jungle outpost was becoming more complicated because of the arrival of child number two. Joy and Steven were one year apart and they definitely needed a lot of attention. As all parents, we were concerned about their daily welfare and health needs. More than once, we entertained the thoughts of what would happen during a severe illness. The local hospital had very limited supplies and the stories of their lack of sterile procedures were in real question.

The closest city was two hundred fifty miles to the north of us in Central Africa where the two children had been born. With no roads leading to the outside world, we could just imagine numerous incidents that could take place. As the weeks passed by, our children were coming down with a number of illnesses, one of which was deadly malaria and perhaps it was the one disease that killed more children in Africa than any other sickness.

We often went to funerals where Gene tried to comfort the grieving parents who were laying their children to rest in unmarked graves in a faceless jungle. There was a feeling of hopelessness and helplessness because we could not do anything more than just comfort them. As we stood daily before the Lord, we prayed, not only for our own situation, but for the condition of all the people living in this hostile territory. The seed was then planted in our hearts about having a health facility one day to care for this population that was like a helpless child.

We had read about many missionaries who had buried their children in Africa. This knowledge would haunt us and place fear in our hearts that we might be among that number who would stand by a little mound of dirt and weep over a precious little one whose life was cut short much too quickly. We knew when we came to this rather unknown and isolated place that there would be many risks to take but now reality was setting in. Battles were being waged in our hearts. Every day, we had to commit these feelings to the Lord because we knew that if we didn't have victory in our lives concerning our children, Satan would use these thoughts to make us ineffectual.

A few weeks before, the young man, Michel, who worked for us in our home failed to come to work one day. By the end of the day, he sent word that we should come to his mud house that was about a half mile from where we lived. Family members were all gathered around a little body that lay on a mat. Candles were lit near the head and women were wailing and throwing themselves on the ground. The little child belonged to our worker, Michel and his wife, Alphonsine. We paid our respects to the family and returned by pedal bike to the mission station. The next morning, my husband was asked to have a brief message before the little one was put in a shallow grave next to their house. As usual, the sun rose very hot the next morning. The air was heavy with humidity and the stifling heat was oppressive. We prepared to go and be a part of the heartache of this family, something that we would see all too often in the ensuing years.

Gene preached a very simple sermon and ended by asking the growing crowd to come to Jesus as He only could heal our hearts and give us that hope that we could someday see our loved ones in Heaven. We had come to a land where people knew nothing about Jesus and His love and plan of Salvation. Being saved from sin was a new concept for them. This was a heathen culture and God had sent us here to share our very lives and faith with them.

The Christian service ended and the village ceremonies took over. The young mother, Alphonsine, was asked to stand at the head of the shallow grave. She wore only a grass skirt and her breasts were bare. This was the typical dress for a funeral. As the drums beat wildly and the chanters chanted words in their tribal tongue, the little naked body was handed to the young fifteen year old mother. According to tribal custom, the young mother was to take the tiny child, wrap it in banana leaves that were handed her and place it in the open grave. As the child was being given to her, she began to weep and wail. She screamed loudly that she was not able to put the small child in the ground. The drums beat even louder and the yelling of orders became more commanding. The women standing nearby pushed her violently and chided her for failing to listen. As we looked on, our own hearts were broken to see what it was like to bury a loved one when there was no hope. No one showed love, comfort or consolation. We knew why we had come. As they struck out at her, the hurt in my own heart knew no end.

The grieving girl stepped forward, took the banana leaves and wrapped the little one inside. It was all so cold, so void of tenderness. I couldn't hold back the tears that were coursing down my face. I stepped forward, placed my arms around her and simply stated,

"Alphonsine, I understand your pain and suffering."

She turned on me in anger and shouted, "White lady, what do you know about burying a child? You have everything."

Weeping uncontrollably, I said, "Oh I do understand. You see, I lost my first child also."

Having said that through a torrent of tears, I turned and ran down the jungle path to the mission station. The raw feelings of grief had overtaken me once again. The sorrow had been locked away in my heart and I hadn't wanted to look at it and deal with it anymore. A few years previous to that time, we were in Bible College studying to go to Africa. The future was ahead of us with all its challenges and hopes of great happiness. We had turned our back on a lucrative job and we were content in knowing that we could go to the ends of the earth together, just so that we might serve the Lord. In our youth, we felt that we could conquer the world and everything that it had to offer. We hadn't anticipated that there would be many mountains to climb and valleys to walk through. Isn't it wonderful that God allows us to live one day at a time? If we saw into the future, we might never serve God or know the rich blessings that He has for those who will take up their cross and follow Him. During this time, we were overjoyed to learn that we were going to have a little one come into our home. We had been told on many occasions that we would never be able to have children. I felt like Samuel's mother must have felt when she learned that God would grace their home with a little child. She wanted that child to grow and serve God. That he did.

It was a beautiful October day in 1953 when our small son came into the world. He was much too small but we knew that God would work it out somehow. The new baby bed was waiting at the apartment and there were little baby clothes to fix him up when we got home from the hospital.

But something was so wrong. Looking at him in the incubator, he seemed so helpless and his little arms were blue. He was beautiful though and the joy of our life. Even though the doctor avoided talking to us and the nurses had sad looks on their faces, it never once dawned on us that this precious gift from God would leave us. Very early one morning, a nurse came into my room weeping. Softly and tenderly, she said that our little son was gone. The words didn't sink in. There had to be a terrible mistake. She couldn't be talking about my child. As the reality of it all sank in, I began weeping until I was completely exhausted. A nurse slipped in quietly and gave me an injection. With that, I slipped into darkness. Hours later, I awakened to see my husband looking down at me. He held me close and our tears mingled together.

Broken in spirit, he went to look for a little casket and satin dress to put him in. Throughout the long night, Gene sat and mourned beside this little lifeless body. Plans were made by our home church to fly us home to Canton, Ohio where we would bury our son in my husband's gravesite. Seeing our families and friends was comforting, but no word of consolation would heal the grief that we felt in our hearts. Bitterness was building inside of me. My husband had relinquished all his sorrows to the Lord during that long, lonely night at the funeral home. He wanted to hold me up and be strong for me, but I could not be consoled. I was to carry the grief and bitterness for a long time before there was complete victory in my soul. The pastor's wife sang, "Safe in the arms of Jesus." The anger was building up in my soul. God was trying to teach me something but I was not listening and I was not willing to learn at that particular time. It would have to wait a long time. Standing together at the grave, we had no idea that God would use this completely overwhelming pain to help hundreds of African women to come to terms with their own sorrow.

A few days after Alphonsine had laid her little one to

rest, she came by the house to see me. She wanted to know what I was talking about when I told her that I understood her grief. Slowly, I recounted my story of loss. I wept again as I relived the circumstances of the death of little Eugene Paul. In the quietness of our time together, I was able to share with her the moving story of Jesus and how God sent His Son to this earth to be sacrificed on a cruel Cross because He loved us so much. He died that we might live. This broke down the stony wall of her heart and she asked Jesus to come into her heart that day. How happy I was that I could share the Gospel because without my hurt, Alphonsine might never have believed. Several years later, while going through another birth, Alphonsine went home to be with the Lord.

I went alone to be with the Lord and there in the privacy of my room, I wept before Him. The bitterness was suddenly gone. It had been locked so tightly in the corner of my heart, but God opened the door and freed me of the weight that I had been carrying. As sad as our experience was, God meant it to be that way so that we might feel the loss and be able to help these forest people who lost their little ones much too often. We had laid our son away in a beautiful casket. These people were laying their little ones away in banana leaves. What a contrast! God had sent us to show them the Way. We both knew that day that we could never turn back no matter what the cost might be. The tom-toms became a way of life in jungle living. Day after day, someone died and the village drums would beat incessantly. Some were so close to the mission and others were in other villages, but the beat of sorrow hammered its throb into our hearts. So often, our little daughter, Joy, would awaken in the middle of the night and she would call out, "Mommy, won't the drums ever stop beating?"

"No honey, the drums will never stop beating. Go back to sleep," we would reply. They would always be a constant reminder to us that life was so short in this land of disease. Death was a daily companion that we would all have to live with. It was also a reminder to us that we had much work to do to point people to Jesus so that instead of dancing and drinking to ward off evil spirits, they might learn to trust in One who would give them life after death. Many, so many, were passing into that shallow grave without knowing Jesus. We could not fail our Lord, we must not under any circumstance. With that great responsibility placed upon us, the Great Commission before us and the peace of God in our hearts, we set our hearts again to the many tasks that lay ahead.

When Moses and the Israelites crossed the Red Sea in their flight from the Egyptians, they paused to worship God and sing a song to God for His protection, His victory, and His love in sparing them from the enemy. Lifting up their voices, they sang this song, "Thou in Thy mercy hast led forth the people which Thou hast redeemed: Thou hast guided them in Thy strength unto Thy holy habitation" (Exodus 15:13). In His strength, there would be nothing too hard for Him. He would not fail us and He would bring us unto His holy habitation.

PLEASE FATHER, DON'T TAKE MY SON

Even though life was difficult on our jungle station, we had more peace and joy than we had ever had in our lives. The mud houses had been torn down and Gene was building brick homes. We and our children would definitely be a little safer. One brick home had been built before we arrived and while our senior missionary was home on furlough, we were able to live in her home. The days held many challenges.

Sandy with an armful of love

Gene and the workmen made brick kilns to make fire burned bricks, they dug foundations, and they often met an incoming river boat with the dugout canoe in order to take tons of cement and roofing from the interior of the barges. This was all done in addition to village Bible classes and Bible school classes. While the days were filled with a myriad amount of tasks, sometimes the nights could take on more duties and responsibilities than we were able to cope with. The heat had sapped our strength, but dry season was coming to an end and we looked forward to rainy nights and the cool air that came with it for a few short hours.

The children had been put to bed and it was quiet and peaceful. We both enjoyed this period before sleep overtook us. The loud hissing of the pressure lantern had been silenced and there was now the loud buzzing and orchestral sounds of thousands of mosquitoes outside the mosquito net. How very much they wanted to get inside to get fresh blood from us.

It must have been sometime after 10:30pm when we heard a faint cry. It was Steven, our son. A pathetic cry came from his little mouth. How could this be when he had been fine at the time that we put him to bed? I bolted from the bed and ran into the children's room. As I gathered him into my arms, I noticed that his body was unusually hot. He was shivering as he whimpered. He had the telltale signs of an acute attack of malaria. I shivered, too, at the thoughts of yet another attack. Rushing to our bedroom, I looked for the thermometer. Pushing back the mosquito netting, we went to work at getting an accurate number on his fever. As we turned his body, he screamed in pain. Malaria not only gives a high fever, it also creates much pain in the joints and considerable body chills. The French doctor needed to look at him immediately. Back in the United States, an ambulance would have been dispatched very quickly, but in the jungles, there was a constant reminder that we had left those modern ways behind us. Outside our room, there was intense darkness along with strange jungle noises. What could we do? Gene decided in an instant that he needed to go on his pedal bike down through a stretch of jungle to the government hospital. It wasn't exactly a fun thing to think of since there was that quarter mile area between us and the village. A man on his bike, with a dog running alongside had been knocked over several nights before by a large leopard. This path was used often by leopards that went down to the river's edge to drink.

I watched him as he departed. My emotions and thoughts were scrambled. It seemed the emotions were running rampant and taking control. It was easy to teach about faith but it wasn't always easy to act on the faith that was deep in our hearts. Facing a life-threatening situation with my son was too much. My stomach felt like huge knots were growing inside. Holding my son in my arms, I sensed that the rigid little body was getting hotter. Once again, I took the temperature and it was a hundred and five degrees. Carrying him out on the veranda, I waited for some sign that Gene might be returning with the doctor. Standing in the partial darkness of the night lantern, I felt his little body become limp. A scream emerged from my lips just at the time that I saw some form of movement at the end of the long path. Gene's bike was emerging from the shadows of the night. No one was with him. He was riding all alone! In the lantern light behind me, he got a glimpse of agony on my face. He threw down the bike and hurried up the steps and took the now lifeless body from my shaking arms. His words were all jumbled as he tried to explain that the French doctor had left that morning to go on a river trip to treat many children with measles. So many had died already and the situation was becoming more serious day by day.

Our bedroom was the place of prayer and we hurried by the bed. This was a hopeless situation that we were facing, one that we could not deal with on our own. Surely, God would meet with us in our very special sanctuary. Gene put the child across his legs and we both wept and wailed before the Lord. God had taken our first son years before. Would He now take our second one? It appeared to us that Steven was dying and we were helpless to do anything. In those gripping moments of time, Gene began to pray and quote Scripture to our Heavenly Father, words that echoed to us from centuries gone by (Jeremiah 32:27). "Behold, I am the Lord, the God of all flesh: is there anything too hard for me?" In a strong and anguished voice, he followed this verse with another challenge and wonderful answer from our great God. Jeremiah 33:3, "Call unto me, and I will answer thee, and show thee great and mighty things, which thou knowest not." He pleaded before the Throne of God. Hot tears fell from our faces onto the small body of little Steven. Surrendering ourselves to a Holy God, we relinquished his life to the will and love of a merciful God.

In the quietness of the jungle night, we waited on God and sensed His arms of love around us. Ever so slightly, the little body moved. My whole being was quivering from fright and fear. We watched him in wonderment. He sleepily opened his eyes and looked up at us. His glazed eyes looked deeply and intently on our faces. The fever was instantly gone. God had performed what no man could ever do. We had seen God's power at work and He was going to allow us to live many years to tell this story of His mighty hand upon us that one very dark night in our lives. From that time until the present, our son has never had another such violent attack of malaria.

The owls were hooting from the palm trees outside our bedroom and the night birds sang their strange refrains as we laid our son in his little homemade bed. He slept twelve hours before awakening at twelve noon the next day. The night had been way too long but we had a song of praise to our Lord because we had been visited by the great God of Heaven. We may have been thousands of miles from the United States and good medical care, but we were just a prayer away from the Great Physician. When all human help was gone, He stepped in to perform a lasting work, not only in the life of our son, but also in our own.

FEAR OF THE UNKNOWN

In a 40-foot dugout

River work became a major part of our ministry. Learning the language was also quite essential if we were going to teach, preach and do visitation. We had to find a place in the hearts of the people. Even though the Bible school had been founded, there was another great priority and that was the rest of the territory, the Likouala Region. There were no roads leading anywhere, only paths and beyond the paths was the river. The dugout canoe was the best way to travel because the thirty-foot dugout could hold several tons of supplies that would be necessary for two to four weeks of living in the villages along the smaller rivers.

Although Gene had traveled at various times with the Bible school students, I had not accompanied him. Our first river venture, together, was a new revelation to me. The villagers had seen the French men who worked for the Colonial Government, but they hadn't seen a white woman before. In several villages, the people ran to the edge of the jungle and hid behind trees when they saw me. With blond hair and light skin, I was something that they needed to study and stare at. To make matters worse, our son, Steven, aged ten months, was with us and they thought that he was even more peculiar. Children cautiously approached him and proceeded to pinch his skin and yank at the little bit of hair that he managed to grow on an otherwise bald head. As time passed and we expanded our river travel, I was to become the first white woman to arrive in all of the far off corners of this vast territory.

We were cautioned before our departure from our mission station that we should be extremely aware that there were powerful witch doctors in some of the villages. We wondered how we would know who they were since all the people appeared to look alike to us. It isn't that we threw all caution to the wind, but we had work to do for God and we would have to depend on Him to guide us, instruct us and teach us in the way that we should go.

Pygmies standing on each side of an African monkey hunter

We were entering into new areas and we would surely face the enemy himself, Satan. It is safe to say that we never met one Christian person in those distant jungle areas. The people were living as they had lived several hundred years before. Their houses were made of mud and the roofs were constructed from a certain kind of river palm that was worked and tied in a fashion that could withstand the wind and the rain. The village women wore colorful grass skirts. The men were attired in loin cloths or soft bark. Some 20,000 Pygmies roamed the jungles but there always seemed to be a group of them living behind the regular villagers to make their gardens or plantations. Most of these Pygmies were unclothed.

A Frenchman, who had been in the area a number of years, built a home along one of these smaller rivers called the Libenga. He owned boats and many barges and he often went up and down the smaller rivers to sell pots,

An old river boat loaded with natives

pans, salt, matches, kerosene and lamps as well as other precious commodities that the villagers needed. Knives, machetes and axes were of great value to them. When this Frenchman died, his barges were left to rust and the traveling store ceased to exist.

The thick foliage of the jungle, along the rivers, was beautiful and full of wildlife. As we rode along, pushed by a twenty-five horsepower motor, we could look deep into the water. It was like a vast mirror that reflected the inner jungle. The water was calm and reddish black due to the rotting trees and perhaps minerals. Hours passed slowly in the blazing sun. Only the humming

Sandy playing accordion

sound of the outboard motor broke the silence. The small tributary was like a snake twisting itself through this paradise. Maneuvering the sharp curves often pushed us into the entangled underbrush of the jungle. Villages were hours apart. No land was seen. Tall jungle trees rose out of the swamp and river to stand high in the air. Trees were covered over with thick vines, a haven for wild fowl, tropical birds and monkeys of many species. Crocodiles were occasionally spotted as they slid off very small areas of sand. Near the underbrush, huge fish and small ones alike leaped into the air as if they were performing for our pleasure. This was certainly an unusual habitat for God's creation. Arriving at each village, we were greeted in much the same way. The people seemed awestruck at this white family. Children gawked at some of the modern supplies of the '50s.

We had a German hand turned voice recorder. When they listened to the voices of some of their family members back at the mission station, natives looked all around the box to find the "spirits" of their family members. We looked on in amusement. Villagers also looked

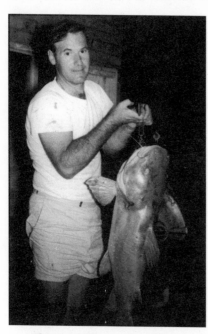

inquisitively at how a white man treated his wife. Their eyes grew large as they watched him take my hand and help me out of the dugout canoe. Assisting me up the thirty-foot embankment and opening a folding chair for me was certainly out of the ordinary. In African society, the woman was made to do the work for their man. It was normal to be mistreated, beaten and ordered about like a slave. True love was a rare commodity. Our way of interacting brought unusual sounds of "ooh's" and "aah's."

Gene caught a large catfish

Each new village, where we stopped, seemed to have its own strange language. This came about, perhaps, because of the long distances between most villages. Unusual as it seems, almost all the people spoke the common language of Lingala. After many years, Lingala would be spoken widely over most of the Congo. Each village Chief needed to know some French so that he could take orders from the French Administrators who often arrived to give out orders for the people. At night, before darkness fell, the pressure lanterns would be pumped up brightly so that we could teach the village children Lingala choruses, songs such as "Jesus loves the little children," "Deep and Wide" and many others. The women would leave their cooking over the open fires and men would sit on the outskirts of the crowd of children. There was a lot of observation. As the fire flickered in the darkness, their eyes grew large as they watched my fingers gliding over the piano accordion keys. The left hand fingers jumped easily over the bass buttons. All this made music.

What a tool for God! Wherever we went, God used the accordion to bring out the crowds of villagers to hear the songs and also the Word of God.

These unusual Bantu people were a giving people who were quick to show their appreciation. They had so little, but such as they had, they were willing to share with us. Some would bring eggs that we used for making adobe cakes, (pancakes). The Chinese kerosene two burner and portable camp oven we brought with us produced some good food. Children came bearing bananas and some of the largest and sweetest pineapples on

Holding pineapple and Steven

earth. Pineapples back there often weighed twenty pounds. Gene laughed as he candled the eggs that we received because there was often a little meat in them in the form of little chicks. This brought sadness to us as we realized that the little chicks in the eggs could have hatched out. This in turn would have given them meat to eat and more eggs. The French allowed the Chief to own a gun, so at times, we were treated to wild pork and ante-

Fried caterpillars are delicious

lope. Feeding our Bible school students who accompanied us meant that much food was needed.

Fish were very abundant in the river, so after dark, Gene and the students would fish awhile to bring in food for the next day's meal. In larger villages, there were chickens and monkeys to buy, the latter being a delicacy for the Bible school students. I must admit that I ate monkey a few times, but it was certainly no great culinary dish for me. After seeing the little head floating in the stew one time, I decided that I could never again eat monkey no matter how hungry I was. Eating unusually strange foods was difficult for me, but Gene learned to enjoy most of them. Village preparation of fried termites was a tasty dish, much like eating salted Rice Crispies. That was the extent of my jungle food. Monkey and fried tree caterpillars were delicacies, but not for me.

I learned to carry noodles, rice and oatmeal to take care of my needs. Vital lessons were learned about living and surviving the rigors of jungle life along the rivers.

Before leaving one village and going on to the next, the Bible school students would warn us that we should not even think of staying in the village of Bangui Motaba. The students were familiar with that village and we wanted to listen to their advice and information that they gave us.

One young student, named Mowawa Eugene, seemed especially knowledgeable about that particular place. He spoke with authority when he advised us to pass by the village. He cautiously stated that it would be better to forget them because this place was exceptionally evil. The people were known to have satanic rites and unusual worship services to their various gods.

After listening to the other stories of horror and ritual, it became our intention to pass by the village and go to a more distant place called Linganga Makao. As much as we feared, it was not God's plan for us to pass by. Darkness fell just as we were approaching Bangui Motaba. Because of the student's warning, we were almost too afraid to disembark and ask for the Chief. When the motor was turned off, we timidly spoke with the villagers and asked them if we might be able to speak with the Chief. Suddenly, he appeared and glared at us in an angry manner. Gene stood tall and asked him if we might be able to stay in the passage house and then have services to teach the people about God. He erupted with a loud roar and with a thundering voice, he told us that we could not because white people stole his people and made canned meat with them. This was news to us. No wonder they feared us. But how would these people hear about God's plan for them? God's Word specifically told us that there was only one way to Eternal Life and that was through believing in Jesus as Savior. What would happen to them and their children? They would never enter into the family of God. Old teachings and customs would forever separate them from the Truth of God.

We explained to the Chief that we did not have lights on our outboard motor and we would need a place to stay for the night. French Administrators insisted that each village build a decent and relatively new mud house that would be kept as a "passage house." The Chief pointed to the house near the water and told us that we could all stay there. It was close to the boat and we were able to quickly carry our supplies to the mud house before total darkness fell.

Before leaving the mission station at Impfondo, one of the students sneaked a little dog into the boat. I had seen it earlier and advised him that it might be wiser if he would leave it behind, since it could be a nuisance and would consume precious food supplies. If we lacked anything, if we forgot anything, it was much too late to think about it. We were many miles from the mission station. There were no stores in which to buy things that we lacked, unless, of course, we happened upon the Frenchman and his boat store. That never happened. Since the old Chief would not allow us to have services, we decided to eat our meager meal, string up the mosquito nets and turn in early. Close to the river's edge, the mosquitoes came in droves. No wonder that so many died of malaria. There was no medicine. Others, however, were evidently resistant or else there would be no one alive. It was survival of the fittest and most resistant.

Before turning in for the night, we gathered to pray. Prayer was offered up for the old Chief and the village as a whole. Our hearts were troubled as we remembered the happenings of the afternoon. Standing beside the Chief had been a young lad. When he heard that we wanted to teach songs to all the children, his heart was touched. He begged his father to allow us to stay on a few days to teach them many things that we had promised. Angrily, the old man hit the lad with the back of his hand and yelled. It was very clear to us that he would never allow us to remain in his village to teach about the living God. The boy stood up, dusted himself, and walked away in tears and sadness.

The mud hut in which we were staying had no doors to close and no windows to latch. The darkness beyond those big openings could be felt. The students had told us before leaving on the trip that we should bring along pieces of cloth and mats to cover doorways and open windows. Without these, we found the people standing idly at the openings peering in as we ate or got ready for bed.

For some reason, the mat at the door didn't seem very safe, so I asked my husband to put two suitcases at the bottom and edges of the mat that covered the door opening. The intense darkness outside was a blackness that we were not used to in the United States. It definitely could be felt and reminded us of the spiritual plight of those people. They were living in heathen darkness and the Light of the Gospel had not as yet penetrated this part of the Congo. Before my husband got into his army cot, he turned the night lantern way down low. Butterflies were in my stomach and a feeling of imminent danger made chills come over me. I whispered to Gene that if either of us heard anything suspicious, we would pinch one another ever so slightly. As I lay watching the night lantern cast shadows on the mud wads, I fell into a very troublesome sleep. From time to time, I awoke and listened. The cries of leopards nearby alerted us that they were on the prowl for village goats and sheep. They almost sounded like a restless baby and, without doubt, were waiting for a good dinner.

Perhaps it was my imagination, but I thought that I heard some shuffling of feet. The noises were near our door that was protected by that fragile mat. Was it real or was I just imagining all this? I sat upright. Fear was there again. My heart pounded as I imagined witch doctors out there with spears in hand. Stories like that were from long, long ago, or so I thought. Nothing like that could happen to us or could it?

My thoughts were running wild. In the next room were the Bible school students. I could hear deep breathing and knew they were oblivious to approaching danger. The footsteps shuffled ever closer. In the students' room, that little dog, that I didn't want to come along on this trip began to growl as if he were being disturbed in his sleep. Was it possible that he was hearing what I heard? The footsteps stopped. I quickly pinched Gene.

He sat upright and listened with me. I pointed to the mat that was no security to any of us. Was it possible that the witch doctors in the village had decided to kill us after all? Had we come so far just to be murdered? We bowed and prayed to ourselves asking God's protection. Suddenly, the little dog began barking loudly waking all the students. The man or men outside the mat began to flee. We had left a lot of supplies outside the door by the mud house and they fell over everything, scattering supplies in all directions. The students were in our room in no time, along with the little dog that God used to make a mighty bark. The little nuisance had become an instant hero. The men ran out into the inky night. One of them called and said that they should all return to the house as we didn't know what plans the intruders might have.

Again, we prayed for protection, imploring God to care for us and rest our tired bodies as we had a long ways to travel the next day. Assured that our Heavenly Father was right there to watch over us, we returned to our cots and quickly fell into a peaceful sleep. All too soon, the sun rose over the jungle and we could hear the children outside waiting for the strangers to appear, especially the strange looking little boy and his mother. It was evident to us that the children were innocent, but there were forces in that village that were evil and sinister. We all had a feeling of what the Apostle Paul must have felt when he was in areas of danger and among people who were hostile to the Gospel.

Our little group packed the dugout once again and pulled away from the shore line. There was a relief in each of our hearts to leave and go to other places where we might be better received. At the end of the Motaba River, we saw a village come into view on a high bluff. Hundreds of Pygmies and village people welcomed us with open arms. Each night, we taught choruses that they could easily learn. So far away, the praises of God were being heard and sung for the very first time. They listened intently to the Gospel story, a story that in time would change the lives of the people forever.

Night after night, we watched as children and older people responded to the simple story of Jesus, how He came, how He lived, His death on the Cross and His glorious resurrection. The simple Gospel and plan of Salvation found a haven in the hearts of many. As we packed our dugout once again, the people begged us to return as soon as possible. The first inroads into this dark area had been made. God was with us. Each of us was ecstatic to see the great possibilities for future service, not only for us but for our Bible school students who would graduate and later become pastors to people such as these. God's Eternal plan was coming into focus and we were ready to take on the challenge. The barriers of pagan darkness were being broken, but it would take years of struggle as a spiritual war would rage between the forces of Satan and God. Satan had held the people in satanic bondage way too long. We were not disheartened. We were equipped to do battle with the enemy. The victory was sure!

NEW LIFE COMES TO AN OLD, OLD VILLAGE

Over twenty-five years passed by. Each time that we passed by the old Chief's village on the Motaba River, we thought about the souls there who had gone into Eternity without ever knowing that Jesus was the Way to Eternal Life. Several years before, God brought to our station Dr. John and Judy Look. They had ministered in another area of Congo, but due to government problems, they left Ouesso, where John was effective as a dentist and Bible teacher.

Gene planned another river trip up the Motaba River and he and John Look felt that it would be a double blessing to the people if they went together. John would take care of the many dental problems among the people, as well as treating many other illnesses. Together, they would take turns preaching Christ to all who would listen.

As they were approaching the old Chief's village, John suggested that they stop. Gene recounted past experiences of how angry the Chief was, that he didn't want to hear anything about God. They both thought that perhaps, after so many years, the old Chief would have a change of heart and allow them to minister to his people. After tying the boat up at the shore, the villagers came and said that the Chief was in the jungle and not available to talk with them. The men explained to them that they were going all the way to the end of the river and in another week or two, they would come back and stop by once again and ask to share, not only the Gospel, but dental care would be given to all those who were in need. If there were sick in their midst, as there always were in the far off places, they would receive treatment and medication. Tropical diseases killed so many. Gene shared that he had a heavy feeling in his heart as he looked at this people, lost people without a Shepherd. Jesus, the Good Shepherd, was waiting to take them from darkness into Life. Because of the Chief's hardness of heart, they might never hear.

The week went quickly as their dugout canoe carried them to each jungle village. The hearts of the two men were overjoyed as they shared the Word of God. Many were accepting Jesus as the Lord of their lives and their newfound faith gave them a hunger to have a pastor among them to tell them every day how they might walk with Jesus. The heathen were being redeemed and the angels in Heaven must have been singing. Jesus said in John 6:40 "that everyone, which seeth the Son and believeth in him, may have everlasting life, and I will raise him up at the last day." This gift of Life had been given to so many. What would happen to the old Chief's village?

At the end of a very long ride down the winding river, the men arrived at the village where a door was about to open very wide. Gene stepped out and asked for the Chief. A younger man stepped forward and said, "I am Alexander, the Chief."

Gene questioned him as to the whereabouts of the old Chief and Alexander said that he had died.

There was a moment of sadness as Gene thought about him going out into eternal darkness, but also a feeling of elation that perhaps, just perhaps, this young Chief might open the door to allow the Light of the Gospel to come in. Gene and Dr. Look conveyed to the Chief that they wanted to treat the illnesses of the people and that they wanted to give them a gift, the gift of the Gospel. Would Chief Alexander allow them the privilege of staying in the village to minister among the people? They couldn't believe what they were hearing. The answer came. Yes, they not only could sleep there but they could stay as long as they wanted to give out medicine and preach the Word of God.

Many people helped them carry the supplies from the dugout to the mud house where they would stay. After their bed gear and footlockers of food, medicine and other things had been placed in the house, the Chief asked that they accompany him to stop at each mud house to tell the people to come to the service in the morning. Gene wondered if he were dreaming. So many years he had passed by this place and now they were being welcomed with open arms. The men had a feeling that God's blessings were yet to be poured out upon them. After eating and praying, the men and some of the Congolese pastors and Bible school students went to bed with happy hearts.

While it was yet dark in the early morning hours, the young Chief came by and asked that Gene go with him again to each house and then back to the Pygmy encampment. Gene was extremely tired and quickly told the Chief that they had gone around the night before. Was it necessary to go again? The young Alexander told him that many had been in the forest the night before and they got into the village very late. Almost all the Pygmies had been gone also but they were now at their village behind the main village. So, once again, all the villagers were invited to come and learn many songs. Gene was going to bring the early morning message from the Word of God. They all were anxious to come and hear what was going to be said. The crowd of villagers sat on the ground. Some carried little stools that they had whittled from soft wood. The children were everywhere, and some government teachers were present as well. The government tried to put teachers in every village so that all children would have the opportunity to learn. With much joy, the children began to learn the songs that the Congolese pastors were teaching them. The African people love to sing and these choruses that they were learning were like new life being poured into them. Happiness and enthusiasm could be seen on the faces of everyone. This was indeed unbelievable.

Because the people had never heard the Gospel, Gene brought a simple message telling about the Creator who had made the world and all that was in it, and then the plan of God to send Jesus to earth that He might live among the people and die on a cruel cross for the sins of all in the world. He ended his message with a prayer on his lips. The Word had been planted as a seed, on hearts that seemed so eager to hear. It was the work of the Holy Spirit to take the message and apply it to each soul present. There was a hush as he prayed and the Spirit of God was moving over the people. They had heard but what were they going to do with this message? Would they turn their backs on this opportunity to open the door of their heart to Jesus or would they invite Him to come in. It seemed as if Jesus was standing there inviting them. He was saying, "Behold, I stand at the door, and knock: if any man hear my voice, and opens the door, I will come into him, and will sup with him and he with me." Revelation 3:20. Quietly, he asked those who wanted to invite Jesus into their heart and life, that they would step forward and stand before the people. He waited as they came. The crowd of people grew larger. It was as if they had waited their whole life for this moment of time.

Because there were so many, Gene and Dr. John divided the people up who came to accept Jesus as Lord. They went to different mud houses where there would be quietness and an opportunity for each one to pray and open up his or her heart to the Heavenly Father.

Gene noticed that the young Chief was in the group. There was something different about him, a touch of longing in his voice and a gentleness that seemed unusual for the conditions in which he had grown up. This village, so far from nowhere, was adding new saints to the rolls of the Heavenly Kingdom.

Suddenly, the muddy, dirty village was changed into a beautiful cathedral for God. His very presence walked among them.

Alexander, the Chief, stood up to speak. Every eye was on him. Every ear was open to listen to every word. With tears welling up in his eyes, he said, "Years and years ago when I was a young boy, a white lady and a white man came to our village. They said that they wanted to teach us to read and sing beautiful songs. But, my father yelled at them and insisted that they leave as he didn't want to hear about their God. My father, who was holding my hand, suddenly threw me to the ground because I begged him to allow the white man to tell us about the Man in the Black Book. I wanted to learn the songs that the white lady talked about. She had a funny thing that she squeezed and it made music. My heart yearned to learn, but my father angrily said, 'No'" As Gene stood listening to this touching story, he said to the Chief, "Alexander, I am that white man that came to you twenty five years ago, and that lady was my wife."

Alexander threw his arms around Gene as they both hugged and cried together. In a tearful, soft voice he cried, "Oh, what if you had given up? What if you had never returned? This day of new life for me and our village would never have happened."

Dr. John and Gene returned down river to the mission station. They were weary in body, but their hearts were singing a new song, a song of great joy for that special day when many heeded to the voice of God calling them to open the door of their hearts to the Salvation that Jesus was offering them, which would result in life everlasting.

That night, as we prayed together, we asked for endurance that we would never give up, no matter how hard life might be in this harsh land. "How then shall they call on Him in whom they have not believed? And how shall they believe in Him of whom they have not heard? And how shall they preach, except they be sent? As it is written, how beautiful are the feet of them that preach the Gospel of peace, and bring glad tidings of good things!" (Romans 10:14, 15).

I SEE HIM COMING FOR ME

There were so many physical needs among the Pygmies and village people. So often, I wished, in the depths of my heart that Jesus would come back and heal all as He had done so long ago when He walked the earth.

One of the students from the Bible school asked us to pray for his wife one day during the class period. He said that she was in the hospital and it didn't appear that she was getting any better. When time permitted, we went to the government hospital to have prayer with her. We learned that she had an advanced case of tuberculosis. Previous to this time, she had accepted the Lord as her personal Savior and she shared her faith with all her friends and family. Our hearts were burdened for her condition, knowing that unless God intervened, she would not be with us very long. After classes were terminated one day, we took communion to her room. Each day she became weaker and if we waited, she would not be able to drink or partake of the bread. The French doctor came to see her on his daily visit with all the patients. He called her husband, Albert, and told him to take her home where she could spend her final days with all her family who loved her. After my doctrinal class one afternoon, a family member arrived and told me to go quickly to visit Albertine. She was not able to speak anymore and they knew that she was going to die soon. Her short life on earth was fast coming to a close. This couple had no children but they had a great family among the church people.

Getting on my pedal bike, I made my way to the center of the village of Impfondo. Many of the villagers had arrived. The women were inside but the men stood outside. The people all greeted me with a nod and said, "Mbote" which meant "hello." I returned the greeting and stooped to enter the small, but orderly, mud house. Mats had been placed all over the dirt floor and the women were sitting all around her weeping.

Some of the family members were wailing as they watched their sister slowly dying. She had wasted away and her frail body showed the ravages of what tuberculosis could do to a normally healthy body. I greeted her but she only looked at me through eyes filled with pain. Violent coughing spasms left her limp and helpless. This sapped all her strength and I could tell that she was ready to be released from the suffering and cares of this present world. There was sudden silence in the room as everyone looked at her peaceful face. We all could see that the Lord of Glory had walked into our midst. With unusual strength, Albertine sat up and looked at all of us in the room. She started to speak in a strong voice that everyone could hear.

"Please, my sisters, do not cry for me." As we looked on in amazement, she said, "Look, Look! He's coming for me. His hands are extended for me to come."

Having spoken these words, she lay back on the mat, closed her eyes and she was gone. Total silence followed. All who heard were awestruck. She had not been a teacher or an evangelist, but that day, she gave forth a testimony that no one in the village forgot. Because of her witness of God's power and testimony about where she was going, many villagers began coming to church, and eventually, many of them came to a saving knowledge of Jesus Christ.

In our culture, this would have been rather dramatic, too. We would have proceeded to bury her and this would have been the end of a beautiful experience. In the culture of the forest people, this was only the beginning of many things to come. The men of the family were to look for those who would beat the tom-toms all night. Those who did not know the Lord would indulge in dancing and heavy drinking of palm liquor. A collection would be taken up in the village for such an occasion. The body would be put on a thatched bed with mats on it and candles would burn at the foot of the bed.

All night long and perhaps the better part of the week, the tom-toms would beat. Village custom is very strong and those who refuse to adhere to the strict laws of the village would be persecuted in some way and even ostracized from the tribe.

Albert, her husband, realized that Jesus was his Lord and Savior and he could not follow the evil ways of the tribe anymore. He had chosen to turn his back on all this and follow Jesus, no matter what the consequences might be. As we prayed with him, we all knew, in part, what the future would mean for him. He was told that he could not wash his body with soap for a whole year. He must let his hair grow and become matted. He would have to wear the oldest rags that he owned, eat his food without salt and sleep on the ground for a whole year. He spoke to the family of his wife and explained, from God's Word that this wasn't the plan of God. Albert opened the Bible and tried, in vain, to tell the family about his wife's whereabouts. He read the passages from John 14:1-4, "Let not your heart be troubled: ye believe in God, believe also in me. In my Father's house are many mansions: if it were not so, I would have told you. I go to prepare a place for you. And if I go and prepare a place for you, I will come again, and receive you unto myself; that where I am, there ye may be also. And whither I go ye know, and the way ye know." After sharing the feelings of his heart, he went away to his mud hut. That night, he returned to the family home of his wife where there was a vigil. The next day, the grave was dug and the missionaries stood by his side as Albertine was laid to rest.

A battle was being waged in Albert's heart. Would he really listen to the Word of God and obey or would he cave in to the evil village practices? As we prayed, God gave him the victory. The days that followed were extremely difficult for Albert as the family and the villagers turned their back on him, just when he needed their comfort and solace.

As time passed, Albert finished his Bible school training and became a pastor. He knew that he needed a wife to stand beside him in the ministry. Perhaps the family and the villagers had seen how faithful he had been to the Lord and would forget all that had transpired a few years earlier.

He asked for permission to return to his village along one of the smaller rivers back in the interior. The Libenga River was a long, twisting waterway that snaked its way to the north where the Congo met the borders of the Central African Republic. Going by dugout canoe, he spent days paddling against the current to arrive at his native village. There, he met with the family and all the villagers to state his desire to have a new wife to join him in his ministry. The Chief recounted to Albert all the events of Albertine's death and he left nothing out. He was quick to point out that Albert had chosen to put aside every village custom concerning death. After the meeting, that was much like a trial, the chief gave the verdict. Until the day of his death, no one could become his wife, even if they wanted to. He had forsaken the ways of their ancestors and he would bear the curse of living alone until the end of his days.

With a heavy heart, Albert returned to Impfondo. He took a church and began his ministry for the Lord. Years passed by and his only true family was the family of God and missionaries. When he was ill, we came to his help and paid for his medicines when he was in the hospital. Instead of a wife making a garden so that he could come home to a hot meal at the end of the day, he himself worked long hours on Saturday in his jungle garden to care for all the various crops. After dark, he returned with firewood to start a fire to cook his evening meal. He became very thin and weary but he plodded on year after year. There seemed to be no one among the family members who would share with him some of their food that they had prepared. He is old now and quite feeble. More troublesome is the fact that he lives so far from his garden and it is difficult for him to walk such a distance. When we last saw him, he was ill with malaria. We took him to the government hospital, bought his medicine and made sure that he was well taken care of. He was so grateful and soon he was on his way to a good recovery. It is hard to believe that his people would never let him forget that he turned his back on village customs. Never has he turned his back on the Lord but remains faithful to the One who gave him Life.

Albert has paid a high price for putting Christ first and refusing village customs. We wonder if anyone will come to help him when it comes time for him to die. His one hope is the family of God at the church.

Matthew 16:24-26 tells us what Jesus said to his disciples. "If any man will come after me, let him deny himself, and take up his cross, and follow me. For whosoever will save his life shall lose it: and whosoever will lose his life for my sake shall find it. For what is a man profited, if he shall gain the whole world, and lose his own soul? Or what shall a man give in exchange for his soul?"

I wonder if we are willing to leave all to follow Jesus. It means turning our back on many evil practices in this world that we might gain Eternal Life. The answer is found in the depth of our soul when we make a conscious decision to surrender all that we are and all that we have to God. "Behold, I stand at the door and knock: if any man hear my voice, and open the door, I will come in to him, and will sup with him, and he with me" (Revelation 3:20).

WHAT IS LOVE?

In the beginning years of the ministry, we realized that a number of things would have to be implemented. Most of the jungle people could not read. A literacy program was under way when we arrived and it needed to be enlarged upon in order to meet the needs of the vast area of the Likouala Region. With so few missionaries, we would have to have a Bible school to train national pastors who would then be sent to the far away areas of the territory. In 1956, my husband set up a four-year Bible school. We obtained the complete curriculum of our own Bible College in South Carolina and studied it for some time. This would be a tremendous undertaking since we would have to teach in the native language of Lingala. French was taught in the local schools, but we had no highly trained young men who could step into a Bible school that used the difficult language of French.

We did have the whole New Testament translated into the Lingala language. There were also the first five books of the Old Testament as well as Psalms and Proverbs. The young men who wanted to come to the school were relatively new converts. Most had grade school but no high school. The majority of them were ignorant of the truths of Scripture. We were indeed walking into a whole new experience. We used our own Bible school materials that we had taken to the field and much from Moody Bible Institute to begin our translation work for the various Old Testament Books. A few books were available to us from missionaries who were serving across river in the former Belgian Congo. It seemed like an impossible task, but with God's help and direction, we would begin a life long task of Bible education. The Bible college notes in Doctrines of the Bible, evangelism, church history and many other courses took on new meaning as we translated thoughts and truths into our newly adopted tongue. It was a challenge that we did not take lightly. God would have to be our teacher to instruct us in the way that we should go. The God who had made languages would be the same God who would give us insight and instruction in putting on paper His teachings. In essence, we were asking God to give us the gift of tongues, the ability of learning and speaking a language that was foreign to us at that time. We needed fluency in the tongue and talents to reveal the hidden truths of the Bible. Knowing that God had called us to the forest people gave us courage to proceed with faith in His power to direct us in the way that we should go.

Another phase of the program demanded that the Bible school students be taken to the farther most areas of the region to preach the Gospel. This would prepare them for future church planting ventures. Our goal was to teach leaders so that they might one day take over the work. A missionary's work is to entrust his knowledge to others and eventually work himself out of a job so that nationals might carry on themselves. We began the Bible school in 1956 with 19 young men who were extremely eager to learn God's Word and to share it with their own people.

At that point and time, we could not begin to fathom what it would mean to advance the work of Christ in such a primitive area. We had no roads leading to the outside world. In the immediate area, there were paths and dirt roads in the village and passable dirt roads to other villages during the dry season. Most of the work in other places would be done on the river using large dugout canoes. We paddled sometimes, and other times we used a small outboard motor. Living like they did would require a great deal of stamina, understanding of the people and their culture, as well as a heaping portion of love. Earning their respect meant being a servant. That lesson is difficult for all of us.

Students carrying the gospel

We were thrust back on our Lord who taught us the way to be a servant and how to love the unlovely. Jesus taught us in Matthew 20:26-28 "But whosoever will be great among you, let him be your minister: and whosoever will be chief among you, let him be your servant: Even as the Son of man came not to be ministered unto, but to minister, and to give his life a ransom for many."

At the time, I was teaching the books of first and second Corinthians and I noticed that the students were paying special attention to the chapter on "love," I Corinthians 13. Their faces seemed so puzzled as I spoke about Christ's love for the peoples of the world that He gave himself on a cruel cross for us. Knowing that the culture often dictated who a young man or woman should marry, it dawned on me that they might be confused about the true meaning of love.

I opened up a discussion with the class and asked each one to sit for a minute or so and think of what love really was. I was not ready for their strange responses. Some stated that when a man takes a wife and she obeys him in all things, that must be love. Others went on to say that if a woman makes a garden, has babies for the husband and cooks for the family, this might be love. They then stopped and thought about what they had said. They all came to the conclusion that these statements were probably not the true meaning of love. The last young man named Appolinaire thought a long time before he spoke and then he said, "Madame, we don't really know and understand what the true meaning of love is, but whatever you and Pastor Thomas have between you, that is true love."

I stood before them in silence trying to assess this statement. My eyes filled with tears and I constrained myself to keep from crying. This was the clearest indication that we were a living book before these people. If they were to know our Heavenly Father, they would know Him through us and our daily lives that they scrutinized. The Word of God was coming out of our mouths, but the truth of the Scriptures had to be evidenced in our daily living. For them so many truths would take years to fully comprehend. Village customs were at odds with the Word of God. We came to realize that when they turned their backs on the village customs that were contrary to God's Holy Word, their eyes were opened and they enjoyed the true meanings of a life of victory and joy.

That day, we prayed that we might be emptied of self, arrogance and pride. Taking a lowly seat of service before jungle people and the thousands of forest Pygmies, meant taking on the very person of Christ on a daily basis. There would be no other way to win them to the Savior and teach them the complete life of obedience to Him. We are not given a choice if we desire to live for Christ. We are to take on the New Man and put off the Old Man, and we are commanded to live Godly in Christ Jesus. The guidelines for our earthly travel are laid out for us. We have the option of following Him or rejecting Him. Following Him leads to Eternal Life and the fullness of His joy in us.

"And now abideth faith, hope, charity (love), these three; but the greatest of these is charity" (I Corinthians 13:13).

14

GOD SAVES TO THE UTTERMOST

The air was heavy over the village when we set out from the mission station. Our pedal bikes were stirring up dust as we rode through the almost empty village. Men had gone to fish in the river and women had gone to their jungle gardens to work for the day. As we chatted and laughed, we were not aware of a bent figure near the path until she stepped out in front of the bikes. A dirty old sack partially hid her face as she scurried across the road in front of us. With no warning, she stopped and pointed

Native women hard at work grinding meal

113

a long bony finger at my husband and exclaimed in a scratchy voice, "I know who you are, you man of God. You have come to tell us about Jesus."

With those words, she hurried to the riverbank and seemed to slither down like a snake. We were shaken up, to say the least. This encounter made us think about a lot of things. First, we realized that Satan was aware that we were there and secondly, that he would use fear and anything else to frighten us from being effective in our work for Christ. We were appalled at the woman's face. One eye was missing and the flies seemed to be attracted to the white fluid that was coming from the empty eye socket. What did all this mean?

Eventually, we almost forgot about this strange woman. Yet, we couldn't help but wonder where she lived and what purpose she had in village life.

During our years at Bible College, many missionary speakers came from Africa to tell their stories of God's miraculous interventions and of strange people groups who came to Christ because of the faithful teaching of the Word of God. One such man was Tiny Titcom, who worked with the Sudan Interior Mission. His stories thrilled our hearts as he told of those under the influences of Satan who became new creatures in Christ when they came to Him. We would sit in the Chapel and wonder if those days were over or would we also see God work wonders in answer to prayer.

We hadn't been in the Congo long when we began hearing about the secret meetings of the witches. Just the though of witches gave us an uneasy feeling. Our thoughts conjured up pictures of childhood when we drew sketches of witches flying through the air on broom handles. They, of course, were just images and often they came at the time of Halloween. They had originated a long time ago and had evil events connected to it. But, when the locals talked about medicine men, sorcery or witchcraft, we could only surmise what they were talking about. Sorcery and witchcraft were a part of the fiber of the forest people and perhaps, to a larger degree, much of Africa. People not only feared it, they also were a part of it.

A grandmother in the family went to the witch doctors for village medicine for their bodies and also to have fetishes made for themselves and their children. This was to ward off evil. Little strings were made to put around the wrists or waists of the children. Older people had fetishes made for their necks or waist. From their ancestors, they learned that this was one way that they could protect themselves from the evil spirits or the death of their children. Of course we knew that despite the bracelets, they still died and were sick. This later became a very difficult and prolonged spiritual problem in the church as new believers wanted to accept Christ but keep the fetishes. Many were those who were greatly tested and shunned in the family because they refused the fetishes for their children and themselves. Others tried to hide them under their clothes. Most missionaries who have worked in Africa are aware of the consequences their Christians suffered when they turned their back on village customs.

As the sun was setting one afternoon, there was an urgent knock at the door. This was nothing new. There always seemed to be someone at the door, even before daybreak. Opening the door, I saw an anxious mother carrying her little girl.

The child appeared to be quite ill so I invited them into the office. The mother hastened to tell her story as if there was no time to lose. She had taken her daughter to the Impfondo hospital several weeks before and the doctor diagnosed little Georgine as having advance pneumonia. The mother was very poor and did not have sufficient funds to buy all the medicine that they said that she must have for the five-year-old. After some treatment, they had advised her to take Georgine home where she could die with the family around her. With a sad heart, I informed the mother that we did not as yet have the new mission clinic that we were planning and we only had a limited amount of medicine for our own personal use. The mother looked desperate and very tired. She had come to the only place where she thought she could find help and there seemed nothing that we could do.

My own heart was stirred. I was a mother. I knew what it meant to be told that there was no help. Could I send her back home to let the little girl die? Even though I was powerless, there must be something that God could do to help. I gathered some supplies of Vicks, cough syrup and children's aspirins. When our oldest daughter, Joy, was a baby, we had awakened one night to hear her coughing and fighting for breath. Throughout the night, she was gasping to breathe. We made a funnel of heavy paper. After boiling water, mixed with Vicks, we held her at a safe distance from the steam and allowed her to breathe in the mixture. We continued this all night until the sun rose over the distant jungles. It worked for our daughter, it could work for her as we prayed. She coughed up the mucous that had obstructed the airways and we knew that God heard. Guidance was sought from the Lord. This family did not know the Lord, but surely the Lord Jesus loved them and He was able to do that which we could not do. We knew that these people were steeped in paganism and this was an opportunity to show them the power and love of Jesus.

Every morning and every night, the mother brought little Georgine to the house for her medicine and for prayer. Instead of dying, she was gaining strength each day. At the end of the month, we knew that God had answered prayer. This opened the door for us to ask the mother and daughter to come to Sunday school and church services. Sunday after Sunday, the little girl came early and sat on the log that was the bench in the small mud hut that was used for Sunday school. She learned the songs quickly and was eager to have other children come and learn the songs and memorize the Scripture verses, too. After months of faithful attendance, Georgine asked Jesus to come into her heart. Then, she wanted her mother to know Jesus, too. It was now evident why God had spared her life. God knew that Georgine would be with people that we didn't know and she would be able to share the stories that she had heard from the Bible. In this way, all the children could become little missionaries to their own families.

On a bright Sunday morning, we looked out on a happy crowd of people waiting to sing and hear God's Word. African people love to sing and we enjoyed teaching them new songs that they had to memorize because so many of them, in the beginning, did not know how to read. I sat near the front playing the accordion and watching the happy people. One face seemed to glow. It was Georgine. Beside her sat her mother.

When the service ended, I was overjoyed to be able to talk with the two of them together. The mother said that Georgine had been chiding her on a daily basis for not coming to the House of the Lord. Georgine testified to her family that it was God Who had touched her body and made her well again and they should all be worshipping Him together. The message finally struck a chord in the heart of Christine, the mother, and it was then that she decided to at least come and listen to what was being said in the big, mud church. What joy it was, weeks later, when the mother also asked Jesus to come into her heart. Even though Georgine was very happy, there was also a sad sound to her voice sometimes when she talked about her extended family. She was very concerned about her grandmother as she loved her very much.

During the week, Georgine went faithfully to visit her grandma and plead with her to come to God's House. Several years passed by and Georgine was growing into a lovely young lady. She never stopped asking for a special prayer request. She wanted her "koko" (grandmother) to come to Jesus. We sometimes become impatient and do not persevere when we pray for others, but this little girl never gave up.

As my husband was preaching one Sunday morning, he noticed an old, bent over woman sitting on a little stool outside the door of the church. The bamboo roofing hung way out over and sheltered her from the blazing sun. A cloth covered her head and only half of her face could be seen. Before he finished praying at the end of the message, she got up and disappeared. We had no idea who the woman was but we began praying for the little, unknown lady who came and then disappeared. Gene decided that he would do something different the next time that she came. Before he came to the end of the service, he stopped and asked the hunched back lady to come inside the church. She looked up at him from behind a part of the cloth and said, "Oh white man, I cannot come into the church. I am not worthy to come into God's House. I am too wicked." With those words, she picked up her little stool and fled down the road. With tears in my husband's eyes, he said, "Which one of us is worthy to come into His House?" For God's Word says in Romans 3:23, 24, "For all have sinned, and come short of the glory of God; Being justified freely by his grace through the redemption that is in Christ Jesus:"

Over a year passed by and the little dried up woman continued to come listen and depart quickly. She never came inside the church to sit with the rest of the congregation. Our prayer never ceased in her behalf. Because of it, a wonderful answer was on the way. The mud church was becoming too small as the numbers of people increased each week.

Some 500 people packed the humble worship place on this particular Sunday. This day was bound to stand out in our memories because the message was about Jesus picking up the lowliest of humanity, loving them and dying for them. At the end of the message, there was an altar call for the sinners to come unto Jesus. It seemed as if Jesus' arms were extended, saying, "Come unto me, all ye that labor and are heavy laden, and I will give you rest. Take my yoke upon you, and learn of me; for I am meek and lowly in heart; and ye shall find rest unto your souls. For my yoke is easy, and my burden is light" (Matthew 11:28-30).

The service ended and it seemed that no one would come unto Jesus that day. At the end of the prayer, the little woman was standing outside the bamboo. She had not fled. As my husband approached her, she stood silent. With stumbling words, she indicated that she wanted this Jesus to come into her life and wash away all her wicked ways. Gene called me that I might take her to a quiet place to talk with her. This little humped back lady's life was hanging in the balance.

Behind the church and in the quietness of the hour, the crowd of villagers departed, but she and I remained alone with God. From her mouth came the most shocking events that I have ever heard. She recounted to me that she had made medicine to kill many people and that their blood was on her hands. She had been one of Satan's faithful workers in destroying the lives of so many villagers. She wanted to know how God could ever forgive her for all the wicked acts that she had committed. I shared with her the most wonderful words that we could ever hear and they were, "That if thou shalt confess with thy mouth the Lord Jesus, and shalt believe in they heart that God hath raised him from the dead, thou shalt be saved. For with the heart man believeth unto righteousness; and with the mouth confession is made unto salvation" (Romans 19:9, 10).

God's Word had found a resting place and one more lost soul was brought into the Kingdom of Heaven that day. She finally confessed that it was she who had pointed her finger at us that day on the dusty road of Impfondo. This was the evil witch doctor that was feared by all. Now, she had become a new creature in Christ Jesus. Returning to her broken down mud hut, she brought out all her fetishes, placed them in a pile and burned them. The past had been put behind her because of the wonderful Grace of God. She had nothing of value on this earth, but she was wealthy in that the Heavenly Father had prepared a mansion in Glory for her. This was a living story of God's great love and forgiveness and a picture of heathen redeemed.

HELP, PLEASE HELP ME

Rainy season was a welcome time as the nights were cooler and sometimes the days were more pleasant, especially when the wind was blowing up a storm. Our jungle post, being a little above the Equator, was often like a pressure cooker. Sleeping on the cement floor was the coolest alternative since fans were not available.

The Ubangui River, that was located in front of our mission station, was a beautiful portrait. Beyond was a small island, backed by the jungles of the former Zaire. The beauty of that green wonderland masked the secrets that were within. Those who lived and walked inside knew the realities of the diseases, the poisonous snakes and the wild animals. Some of the beautiful butterflies and flowers made the new sub species lists as people from all over the world came to search for something new. Often, we would stand on the river bank in the evening and marvel at God's beauty. One morning, the beautiful blue sky began to turn gray and then to a black and boiling mixture of clouds. Turmoil and fury were to be unleashed. It was a good indication that this one was going to be ugly and ferocious. The wind picked up speed and howled like a wounded bear. White caps on the water peaked and revealed the deep troughs of troubled water. Our boat at the beach bounced up and down like a toothpick. Dugout canoes were being beached, one after the other. Village children began running over to the riverbank to observe the fishing boats that were being tossed about. Some were afraid that family members might be in them. This was terrifying to all of us. In the midst of the wind, some fishermen left the shores on the other side of the river. This they definitely knew was a strategy that had proved disastrous over the years. Yet, they had the feeling that they could probably make it home before the storm's real fury was loosened. Somehow, we think that we can beat the odds. Some do. Others don't.

We make choices every day and often they are the wrong ones. As a part of the observers, we could plainly see that some in the water would not arrive home.

A few dugouts were still on the water bobbing up and down on the waves. One dugout canoe held a fisherman with his grandson who had just arrived by plane that day. Another boat had one old fisherman in it and he was struggling against all odds to fight the wind and the monstrous waves. As we stood mesmerized to the spot, we gazed on a scene that was out of a movie. More children and villagers arrived. This easily could have been a football game where the spectators were cheering the players on. The only difference was that this was no game. It was a real life crisis and the lives of a few were hanging in the balance. The cheers rose and fell in an effort to encourage those who paddled the boats. The wind gained in intensity and the waves took on a black, ugly appearance.

Above the wind, I heard the sound of jeeps and looked behind me to see government men jumping from their vehicles. They rushed to my side to ask where Pastor Thomas was. I answered that he was on a river trip and would not return for several weeks. They groaned and uttered their displeasure. When I questioned them, they responded that those people on the river needed someone to save them from certain death. They felt that the pastor would go out to save them. Frankly, I was angry. Since they had very large boats at their disposal, I wondered why they didn't go out on the river themselves. As if reading my thoughts, they responded, "Oh, we couldn't go out there, we might drown. We know that Pastor Thomas risked his life once before to save some young men from certain death, we knew that he wouldn't hesitate to do it again." With that statement, they left in the blinding rainstorm. We pondered their statement.

First it was a strong pelting rain and then it came in torrents, stinging our faces and arms. It was a release for us all. My tears mixed with the rain on my face. All were helpless to do anything. I prayed in my heart that God would be merciful to these people. Across the waves, the men were screaming in terror as they fought to keep their boats upright. The wind was carrying their anguished cries. The winds echoed, "Sunga ngai! Sunga ngai! Bikisa biso!"

Translated: "Help me! Help me! Save us!"

Even though I was soaked to the skin, I could not bring myself to leave this scene of tragedy. The angry waves carried the one boat up in the air and turned it over. The men went under. Children on the shore screamed as they watched them disappear beneath the black water. Suddenly, they came up swimming and they continued to cry, "Save us!"

Over and over, they went down and each time, they surfaced to fight against the stormy deep that beckoned them. Over one hundred children and adults stayed on to cheer the swimmers that they might not give up, but win this battle of death. When it seemed that they might be saved, a killer wave threw them into the air like a soaked rag doll and then slammed them down below the ugly waves. Our breath was sucked in as we waited for them to break the waters again. Nothing happened! The two men had become too weary. They had gone down for the last time. Their battle was over. The final cry for help went unheeded. "Save us, O save us!"

Our attentions were turned to the one last swimmer. He was an old fisherman who had fought the rivers and the storms many times over the years. He knew how to battle this enemy and win. His shiny, black body was making excellent headway and he was inching ever closer to the shore. I wept aloud as I watched in terror.

The crowd yelled, "You can do it. You can do it!"

He was just about to reach shore. Safety was within his grasp. Angry waves again lifted him up. They should have thrown him on the sandy shore. But, fifty feet from the shore, the old fisherman went down beneath the churning fury of the water. He never resurfaced.

The Ubangui River had claimed yet more victims. Each one had been lost forever. Not one Christian was among the lost. In my despair, I turned toward the house, two hundred fifty feet away. In my heart, God's Word echoed in my ears, Luke 19:10 "For the Son of man is come to seek and to save that which was lost." We were there to give them this message but it had not reached them. They not only sank into the deep, they had entered into a Christless Eternity. All hope for them was gone. During the night, I could hear their cries for someone to help them. I saw them sinking down to the bottom grasping for a hand that was not there. Their faces were contorted in fear of death.

This incident was a vivid reminder that our work was just beginning. Thousands of jungle people had not heard the Good News. That is why Gene was gone that day. Living in adverse situations, he was determined to reach the unreached with the only hope that mankind has—a belief in Jesus and the Salvation that He provided so long ago.

As I had prayed for the men to fight the waters to arrive at the shore, I knew that we too had to fight. The task was greater than we were. No matter what came our way, we were to persevere for the Lord. 2 Timothy 2:1-3 reminded me, "Thou therefore, my son (or daughter), be strong in the grace that is in Christ Jesus." "And the things that thou hast heard of me among many witnesses, the same commit thou to faithful men, who shall be able to teach others also. Thou therefore endure hardness, as a good soldier of Jesus Christ."

Ministering in this difficult area would mean suffering. As the years passed, we saw that suffering with Him would bring forth fruit that would remain.

THE LITTLEST FLOWER

Ten years after our son was born, God brought into our home a wee little daughter. The time surrounding this event was most unusual. The year was 1967 and we were coming to the end of Bible school before the vacation break. It was June and we were both extremely tired from the nine month period of studies and activities that come with a school. I came down with a severe case of malaria just as I was entering my seventh month of pregnancy. This was not good news because the malaria cure would often bring on labor. Communism was in full swing and along the way, the government had brought into the country many Russians and Chinese. No good thinking Russian would ever have chosen to come to the jungles to do doctoring, but in this case, they had no choice. They were chosen for the place they would serve. As one Russian doctor later told us, their authorities would ask them if they would like to go to the Congo. Before they could say, "No!" they were told that they would gladly be appointed.

Doctors Mr. and Mrs. Portnoy were sent to our area along with teachers. As usual, the local government officials would bring all white newcomers to the mission station to introduce them to us. The officials knocked on our door and I greeted them all. When the officials told the doctors that we were Americans and missionaries, they backed up and did not wish to enter. The Congolese assured them that it was okay and that we were very kind and gentle people. With much hesitation, they came in. Others who had come along with the official, looked about, and seated themselves in the living room. I prepared refreshing tropical juice mixtures that were always a hit on such hot days. When we offered them the refreshments, they were very hesitant and said that they didn't care for anything. Knowing that Russians were suspicious of Americans, I immediately sensed that they thought we would poison them.

Dr. Portnoy and a friend

After the Congolese had taken their cookies and juice and enjoyed seconds, the doctors decided that maybe it would be safe to have some. That was our first contact with people of that nature. In spite of their uneasiness, and their demeanor, there was something about them that we liked. They would later become very close friends of ours. They were both very concerned about my pregnancy, especially in a jungle atmosphere. When they met our other two children, they were somewhat amazed and relieved at the same time that we would live there and enjoy life. Being troubled so much with malaria, my secret fear was that I would come down with fever and lose the baby.

My fears were realized one day when chills and fever took over my body. Deep in my heart, I knew that I could not carry the baby to term. I had been restless all night and the many aspirins that I had taken did nothing to

The littlest flower — Patty, our youngest daughter, born at only 2 pounds

reduce my fever. I would have to begin the malaria treatment. The Russian doctor came to see us and said that it was not a matter of saving the baby's life anymore, it was a matter of saving my life. I was becoming dehydrated and very weak. The treatment was begun and I went into labor. Around 8:00 a.m. on June 13th, little Patricia Sue was ushered into our home. Present were the Russian doctor, a French doctor, a Congolese midwife and her husband. This man would later become a doctor and be the director of the largest hospital in the capital, Brazzaville. The baby delivered at two pounds on our dining room table. She was bluish and wasn't breathing. The doctors finally gave up and the midwife took over. Gene sat by my side and prayed. The Russian doctor said that she would die and that my husband should prepare for that. When Gene told him that he was going to pray for God's intervention, he scoffed and told everyone that he was an atheist and did not believe in miracles. God was put to the test.

The French doctor took a metal saint from his pocket and handed it to Gene and told him to put his faith in it. He said that he had done that during the World War II. Gene returned the saint and stated that he would rather that God would take the baby, but he would not place his faith in a metal saint. He and others there were mystified concerning these statements. The midwife continued doing her work and performing mouth to mouth resuscitation. The quietness was broken by the sudden cries of little Patricia. All sighed and great relief was felt by everyone.

Each medical personnel knew that the baby was in grave danger. In this isolated place, there was no incubator and no oxygen. Her chances of survival were very slim. With heavy hearts, we wrapped her in rolls of cotton and rolled bandages to keep in the body heat. We looked for a large shoe box. We could put her in this and then in another box with mosquito netting over it. Then the work to save her began. Every three hours, we gave her milk pumped from the breast. This was transferred to a doll's baby bottle. We clipped the end of that so the milk would drip out a little faster. Night and day, every three hours, we carried on this rigid schedule for six weeks until she began to gain a little strength and a few more ounces. Her two pounds of weight would not rise very quickly. A very close vigil would be required if she was to survive. During

The Thomas family poses on the couch

this frightful time, we kept clinging to the promises of God. At three months, she only weighed nine pounds. Any illness or malaria could quickly snatch her away from us.

The Russian doctor marveled at what he had seen. At her birth, he had suggested that we let her die as the struggle to keep her alive was too great. What he saw at three months was a little, but wiggly baby. This was the beginning of a change in his Marxist heart. In an absolutely impossible situation, God had stepped in and showed them all that their efforts were human and feeble. His power had left them in awe. Several days after the baby's birth, I penned the following poem.

> It was just the other day
> That we strolled amongst the flowers.
> We laughed and merrily sang as we
> Chose which one would be ours.
> Of course we chose the biggest one
> Because it was so bright,

We forgot about the little ones that were within our sight.

Do you, as we, look proudly at the stately and the strong?

Forgetting that the weak and small all to the Lord belong?

God came to visit us this week to teach us of His power,

He revealed His might, His love and grace through a wee, wee flower.

> He came so early in the morn,
> His Presence gloriously shone,

And left a tiny rosebud
To grace our humble home.
The wee flower is our baby,
A precious gift that must
Be always kept beneath His wings
That she in Him might trust.

Several years passed by and the doctors never ceased
to be amazed at what God had done. Because of the frequent visits of the Russian doctors, we were able to talk to
them about God. Knowing that the Marxist population
didn't believe in God, we felt compelled to share our faith
with them. The small Russian group was looking hard at
us to see what made us so different. As we shared our testimony with them, they soon were open to listen and
learn about the Bible. Sometimes it was difficult since we
were Americans and they were Russian and we were con-
versing in French. In the evening, after they had shared a
meal with us, they asked that we sit at our organ and sing.
On more than one occasion, we asked them why since
they could not understand a word that we sang. With
longing looks on their faces, they simply answered, "Sing,
just sing to us!"

After three years, the Russian Embassy in the capital
city informed them that their tour of duty was over. We
wanted to give them a gift that would be life changing.

In haste, I sent a letter to Germany to missionary,
Marilyn Haueter, and asked her if she could find a
Russian Bible. Weeks passed by and one day, a notice
was delivered to our door from the Post Office that
there was a package to be picked up. It was a Russian
Bible! Scrambling through the barrels, we found some
beautiful Christmas wrapping paper from America. The
couple was sent an invitation for Sunday evening dinner. They accepted gladly and came as they were starving

for fellowship. While sitting comfortably in the living room, we handed Mrs. Portnoy the beautiful Bible. She paused and then opened the package slowly. As the words of the Holy Bible appeared before her eyes, the tears began to well up in her eyes and slip slowly down her tired face. She noted that it was fully translated into modern Russian that she could read and understand.

Quietly, she began her story of years gone by, a story of pain and suffering. She reached back into childhood and some happier memories of her beloved grandma who had taken her to church. As a child she always wondered what was in that big, black book that was on the table at the altar. As she grew into a young woman, she was forced by the State to join the Communism Youth Organization. The youth went to churches to disrupt and destroy. Yet, there was a gnawing in her heart because of her earlier training and the big, black book. That night, we stood on the veranda and watched them walk down the path together. We were convinced that God was speaking to their hearts.

Soon, it was time for them to leave and we went to the airplane that had landed on the grassy airstrip. They both hugged us and she said that she had sewed her Bible into the lining of her winter coat that she was taking back to Russia. Mr. Portnoy turned to Gene and said that he was an atheist when he arrived in Congo but as he was leaving, he did believe in God. He stated, "I have seen Him in your lives."

They boarded the plane and returned to Russia. We received several letters that had been sent from a tourist depot, but then the letters stopped. They were not allowed to give us their address as they were afraid.

Only God knows where they are today, but we are assured of one thing, they took with them the Word of God that would explain to them the way of Salvation. We have prayed for them over the years and believe that somewhere in their native Ukraine, they may have found a missionary or a pastor who may have befriended them and brought them to the Lord.

The new Russian Bible that we gave to them would surely be used to speak to their hungry hearts. God's Word was so powerful. It had changed the lives of many Congolese and by faith we knew it would change theirs. "For the word of God is quick, and powerful, and sharper than any two edged sword, piercing even to the dividing asunder of soul and spirit and of the joints and marrow, and is a discerner of the thoughts and intents of the heart" (Hebrews 4:12).

God's Word will not return unto Him void and we are convinced in our hearts that His all powerful Word will produce fruit in the lives of this couple who had been sent to the jungles of Congo. All the Russian and Rumanian couples who lived in the area received a Bible in their language. The doors were swinging wide for us to minister to those that God had sent our way from other countries. It will be revealed someday what our love and witness to them accomplished. We pray there will be Eternal results!

17

MOMMY, DO WE HAVE TO GO?

It was the late '60s and the Congo was deeply embroiled in Communism. The Chinese and North Koreans seemed to be everywhere. The fate of many church groups was hanging in the balance, as well as our own. Young people wanted to come to church but they were hindered by those who were in charge of the Pioneers, a Communist organization for young people. All too often, a truck would drive up to the church door and insist that all young people get in and be indoctrinated at the newly

With books in hand, ready for school

built Pioneer camp at the end of town. If they refused to go, they were thrown in the truck.

Our two oldest children were in fifth and sixth grades and they were onlookers to these fearful scenes that bordered on violence. Our son, Steve, who played in the village with his friends was being harassed and called a bad Capitalist, or a neocolonialist. Coming home, he would cry and ask why he should be called bad names when he was born in this land. None of the children had any knowledge of the meaning of these names, but they had heard them often at government rallies and so it was appropriate to mimic the men in power.

Joy was a year older than her brother and she stayed at home. She was very sensitive and didn't want to confront the adults or children concerning all the name-calling. The country was changing for the worse and the relaxed and memorable days gone by were turning into a nightmare. Military groups were doing target practice across the road from the mission houses, in spite of the fact that they had a target range several miles from there in the

Militants marching and waving their flag

jungle. A Cuban led the young militants who were arrogant and filled with a newly given power to confront foreigners or anyone who might have an ideology other than their own. The Church, it seemed, would have to soon take a stand against the abuses.

Our last daughter, born prematurely, had to have a great deal of care and we both knew that there would have to be some painful changes take place in our home. What could we do to protect our children? Each morning, as we started school together, we prayed and asked God for guidance.

Late at night as the children slept peacefully in their beds, we asked God to help us in selecting a mission school for them. There was no other choice. They would have to go away to school. After contacting the Baptist Mission in the Central African Republic, the school council agreed to take our two precious children. They would receive excellent training and be with their peers. They would also be with other missionary children, and at this point in their lives, they needed this kind of fellowship. They would be beyond the sound of guns and the marching of the military each morning at 4:00 a.m. The taunting would cease, it is true, but they would be absent, absent from home and absent from our table. Only other missionary parents will understand the agony of heart that a parent has at this time. I made new dresses and shirts and we worked hours on end to sew nametags on every piece of clothing.

Now, the time had come. The suitcases were packed and every item on the list was checked off. The little red speedboat that we had received from the American Embassy, when they departed from the country, was much too small to carry three people, heavy suitcases and reservoirs of gas. Before the sun broke over the jungle horizon across the Ubangui River, we got up and carried their heavy luggage to the boat. The moment had come and I felt devastated. They had two hundred and fifty miles to go to arrive at the next country. We knew the many dangers of traveling on the river. More than once, our very lives were in danger as our boat rose and fell with the waves during the frequent storms. I remembered the last night, the tears and the words of the children crying out for some answers. Picking up my ballpoint and pad, I wrote:

Goodbye, goodbye dear mother, my young son said,
And with these words, he turned his head.
The tears were streaming down his face,
His fears and sadness, he couldn't erase.

With trembling voice, I whispered a song,
God will be with you all the day long.
He'll never forsake you, you'll not be alone,
Your heart He will enter and make it His Throne.

We commit these dear children to His care and His love,
And know that the angels will guard from above.

Arriving in Central Africa, they traveled by truck several hundred miles more to their school at Kaga Bandoro. As their father kissed them and made ready for the return trip, they asked, "Daddy, will we ever see you again?"

With sagging spirits and a heavy heart, he kissed them and couldn't look back. Although they were only five hundred miles from our jungle station, the trip was long because it was by riverboat and by truck under extreme heat and dusty roads. It seemed to the children as if they had been left at the end of the world. Many years were spent going back and forth to school and the separation never got easier. We stood by the water's edge and listened in silence as the waves whipped up against the shore. My heart sank. The voice of my husband wavered as he prayed that God would go before them, a journey that would last twelve to thirteen hours. It was necessary to stop halfway and get the gas that had been sent on ahead by riverboat. We kissed. We hugged a long time and wept with uncontrollable tears. We were doing the only things that we could do under the adverse circumstances that we faced. The pain was great.

Gene pulled the rope on the Evinrude motor and it sprang to life. Very, very slowly, it pulled away from the shore. Steven had to crawl out to the front of the fourteen foot speedboat and balance the weight for a few miles. When they got up to speed and were able to plane on the water, he returned to his seat. Returning to the house, my heart sank. I was the only missionary on the station. Some were on furlough and others had left due to the critical political conditions of the country. Each month, there were new changes and new fears. Would we be able to stay on and lead a growing church before the marching feet of those carrying the Red Flag? The large meetings with hundreds raising their fists in the air against Capitalism and Democracy made us wonder what they had in mind for us as God's servants.

Entering the house, I sat and cried until I could cry no more. Our frail little daughter Patty lay asleep in her bed. I didn't like being alone at this time. "If only we had a night guard," I thought. The darkness was overwhelming with no lights anywhere and no one with whom I could talk. I picked up God's Word for comfort. I could only turn to my Heavenly Father as I had no answers of my own to stem the flood of feelings that were buried in my heart. In Psalm 55:22, God spoke to me. "Cast thy burden upon the Lord, and He shall sustain thee: he shall never suffer the righteous to be moved." They grew to be young adults and went to high school with most of the children that they had gone to grade school with, but the hurt of being away from one another stayed the same. The empty places at the table reminded us of a decision made years before. The empty cookie jar didn't need more cookies because there was no one to eat them. The sounds of laughter filling the house had grown silent. The void in the heart was never quite filled.

It was furlough time and the older children were leaving the Congo for good. They were going to remain in the United States, finish their last year of high school and go to college. They had grown up much too fast. They had spent more time away at school than at home. Other Godly house parents and teachers had had a large part in shaping their lives. We wrestled for years after with our decisions. Yet, we could not have allowed them to stay under military force and hate the adopted country of their birth.

As furlough was completed and it was time to send our last daughter away to school, the wounds were reopened. She was only seven. The station was empty of other missionary children. She had gone to America speaking and understanding foreign languages such as French and Lingala. At school in America, she was laughed at. It wasn't that they were making fun of her; it was that she spoke with an accent and she did not comprehend the American way of life. Her sentences were backward and her mannerisms were Congolese. Everything was so strange that by the end of first grade, she had to repeat the class again in a Christian school. She needed a good foundation and to move on, she had to understand American people and America itself.

Throughout the ages, missionary parents have had to go through the separation that often broke the spirit of many a child. Perhaps thousands prayed for us and them that they would be happy and content. There is never a substitute for mom and dad but House Parents must be like surrogate parents. We struggled with the Scripture in Matthew 19:29. "And everyone who has left houses or brothers or sisters or father or mother or children for my sake will receive a hundred times as much and will inherit eternal life." Jesus spoke to the disciples, but He was speaking to all who followed in His footsteps.

I thought back to the time when Gene and I first met at Muskegon, Michigan. It was a youth camp with many young people from good Christian churches. A heavy missionary theme permeated the camp. On the last night of the meetings, several hundred young people, from my state, sat on the sand listening to Dr. Sidney Correll, a great missionary statesman who thrust forth a challenge to serve God. A full moon rose high over Lake Michigan. Nearby, the waves lapped gently against the sandy shore. To the front of this large gathering was a bonfire that cast shadows on the faces of these youth, youth that could make a difference in the world. As the challenging message ended, my heart was stirred to the very depths. We were asked to pick up a piece of wood, signifying our life, walk forward and throw it into the fire. This was a sign that we were willing to die to self and take up the challenge of the Great Commission, that we would forsake all that we might carry on the work of many missionaries who had gone before us. Romans 11 told of martyrs who had given their lives for the Gospel's sake. Outside of the water stirring the golden sand at the edge of the water, silence filled the air.

Gene and I held a piece of wood. What would we do with it? We had just recently met and did not know that God would bring us together to serve Him for the remainder of our lives. As the Spirit of God moved on hearts, we went to stand before the embers. The wood was crackling and sending up a sweet smelling perfume before the Lord as we threw in our small pieces of wood.

Silently, we waited as we looked deep into the embers, embers that have forever etched the call of God on our lives. We turned and sat down, moved by the important invitation we had just responded to. Deep in our hearts, we saw a glimpse of what God wanted from us. He would never be content with a portion of our lives. He wanted all or nothing at all. We answered Him that night. Whatever He would ask of us, we would do. Wherever He would call us, we would go. To turn back was not an option. It was settled at the Throne of Grace.

With thoughts rambling through my mind, I realized that God had called us to make the ultimate sacrifice that those who had never had an opportunity might hear. Our suffering would not be greater than that of our Heavenly Father. He had sent His only begotten Son into the world where most received Him not. They had followed Him that they might be fed. They had sought Him out that they might be healed. They had listened to Him sometimes that they might ridicule and mock Him. He was the Son of God and was chosen by God to be put on a cruel cross. He had set His eyes toward Jerusalem knowing that His time had come and He would not fail His Heavenly Father. Jesus had gone before us. He had made straight the way. There was no burden too great that He could not carry, and no separation, no sickness, no lack and no heartache that He could not understand.

Isaiah 43:1b, 2, 3, "Fear not: for I have redeemed thee, I have called thee by thy name; thou are mine. When thou passest through the waters, I will be with thee; and through the rivers, they shall not overflow thee: when thou walkest through the fire, thou shalt not be burned; neither shall the flame kindle upon thee. For I am the Lord thy God, the Holy One of Israel, thy Savior."

ENEMIES OF THE NIGHT

Living on the mission, that was nestled on the edge of the jungle, was almost like living on the farm. We sometimes raised sheep, goats, pigs, ducks and chickens. I say, sometimes, because we didn't raise all of those animals at the same time. We found that sheep love to eat certain kinds of beautiful flowers, as do their cousins, the goats. Pigs that are within very strong fences have a knack for digging under the fences to get out. Their knack went further than that.

When my husband was on a lengthy river trip, they must have had some inside information about it because it was then that they chose to begin their archeological digs. All too often, the time would be on Saturday afternoon or Sunday when there were no station workmen. They didn't choose to stay close to home, they wandered to the villagers' gardens and looked for tastier morsels in someone else's place. The mama pigs also found deliciously succulent and tender food in their new born babies. Gene always watched them carefully near the time of delivery because pigs are often prone to eat their young as do certain kinds of cats. I began to think that if anything could go wrong, it would begin when Gene was absent. Nothing ever seemed to go along on schedule when he took off in that huge dugout canoe for the back country. Why couldn't life be normal just once when he was gone? After a very long and tiring journey along the narrow waterways, he was ready for a few days of rest and relaxation. That evening, I though that I would go to the chicken house and gather the eggs instead of asking Gene to do it. Dark was just settling in when I stepped into one section of the house. I never felt at ease when doing this job because I knew that dangers lurked everywhere among the shadows.

The chickens had done a good job that day and so I enjoyed gathering up all the eggs in each nest. I felt a tinge of fear as I noticed that the majority of the chickens were outside in the dark. This was definitely not their usual habit. They acted a bit squeamish as they looked at the door that they wanted to enter, but didn't. I cautiously entered the chicken house and carefully scrutinized the straw that had been scattered on the floor. There seemed to be nothing out of order. Only two hens were sitting on the roost and that was odd, really odd. Having filled the bowl with eggs, I exited and returned to the house. It was time for the evening meal.

During the dinner hour, I didn't mention what had taken place. It was probably insignificant anyway. Suddenly, a very strange sound was heard outside the house, much like a rooster being strangled. Gene rose quickly and ran out the back door. Our largest rooster was flopping around on the ground in a most unusual way and five hens were lying dead nearby. The majority of the chickens were standing in the darkness. Gene returned to the house to look for several powerful power beams. Those were handy items to have on hand where we lived. Darkness was real when the lamps or generator were turned off.

Congolese were called to help in the search of the unknown. Gene's heart was pounding so loudly that I could hear it. We seemed to be anticipating some large monster, even though I had been out there a short time before and had seen nothing. Cautiously, my husband gazed into the inky black chicken house. He flashed the light around the floor but saw nothing unusual. Then the high beam was flashed on the ledge of the wall. The roofing beams slanted downward over the cement walls and were always a nice runway for the mice and some rats who enjoyed their own Indy 500 from time to time. The light picked out a slow moving and slithering snake on the ledge above the nests. A pressure lantern brought to the scene made a lot of heat in the small room and the snake felt an urge to move on. He didn't go down the outside wall, but he was coming down the inside wall to the straw a short distance below.

Cobra killed in chicken house

A small crowd was gathering, trying to peek in to see this drama that was unfolding. Someone yelled that it was a black cobra and slammed the door shut. With flashlight in hand, the door was again cracked slightly to peer at the invader who was now rising up and swerving from side to side. He was out to sink his venom into the closest person. This called for a battle plan. There was only one thing to do. We needed to have one person open the door slightly while another person threw a spear through the snake. Who would have the courage to step inside and put the spear in the proper place? A young Bible school student, named Bandama Auguste, agreed that if someone would open the door for him, he would enter and throw the spear. Gene opened the door with extreme caution to see where the cobra had positioned himself.

There he was, near the door. He was waiting like a thief in the night. Realizing that he was cornered, there was no way that he would now leave peacefully. It was a dangerous moment with so many people who had gathered outside in the dark. With bated breath, we shivered at the thoughts of what this creature could do if allowed to leave through the open door. Some thought it would be better to allow him to leave but we argued that he could return and the next time, there might be a more serious incident. No, it was better to settle the score once and for all. Again, the door was opened slightly. Bandama poised himself to throw the sharpened spear. With all the strength that his small, lean body could muster, he threw the spear that would end the life of this venomous serpent. The small group outside cheered and we all exhaled the breath that we had been holding. The incident was over, well, that was until the next time. Before going into the house, Gene took his flashlight and scanned the edges of the jungle. This he did every night. He often took his air rifle and killed large civet cats that waited around for a chicken that stayed outside a few minutes too long after the six o'clock hour. They were a greater menace than the snakes. As the strong beam pierced the thick grass by the enormous palm trees, he got a glimpse of a swishing tail. He called the children to come outside and see something really exciting. We heard their screams of delight as they came out the office door.

What surprise did daddy have for them now? They

lived in a hostile environment, but they did not view it as a threat like grownups might. Arriving at their father's side, they excitedly asked what he had found. Again, he put the beam on the tall grass at the back edge of the mission station. He said, "Be quiet now because I think there is a big male leopard kneeling in the high weeds. I will make a shrill noise and he will jump up and flee."

"Okay daddy, do it!" they said.

Daddy shrieked a very loud yell, but instead of slinking off to the jungle, the leopard crouched. All the while, his long tail was batting the grass back and forth in an angry and agitated manner. Gene had not taken this into account at all. He suddenly realized that this large beast could leap and spring toward them. Quietly, he told both the children to back up very slowly in the direction of the house. They did that without another word. Breathless, we sat down and talked about the night's events. It was almost too much for one day. The shelter of the house gave everyone perfect peace. Sitting together in the living room we all took our Bibles out for devotions.

So much had happened that day. We had a time of praise and prayer before the Lord. I had been in the chicken house where the snake was posed above the ledge where I had gathered eggs. Why didn't he strike me? As we talked about all the many possibilities of what had happened, we knew that it was our Heavenly Father who was taking charge over us. It was a daily part of life that we would walk through tall grass, along jungle trails and on sandbars when there was dry season.

Everywhere we went, there were dangers. Serving God and fearing every danger makes an ineffective worker. Paranoia would be a daily partner that would not let us go. Therefore, we had to know who our guardian was and trust Him and our family into His care. Even life in the United States has its fear factors. There is home invasion, murder in unexpected places, open theft of our children and mugging every minute across our country. Our relationship with God, will ultimately reveal how much we trust Him for every aspect of our personal life and family. To serve God is to trust Him completely in all areas. It is necessary to be free from the daily reminders of danger and fear.

David, the Psalmist, reminds us in Psalm 121 that we have a constant Guardian.

"I will lift up mine eyes unto the hills, from whence cometh my help? My help cometh from the Lord, which made heaven and earth. He will not suffer thy foot to be moved: he that keepeth thee will not slumber. Behold, he that keepeth Israel shall neither slumber nor sleep. The Lord is thy keeper: the Lord is thy shade upon thy right hand. The sun shall not smite thee by day, nor the moon by night. The Lord shall preserve thee from all evil: he shall preserve thy soul. The Lord shall preserve thy going out and thy coming in from this time forth, and even for evermore."

With promises like these, we need not fret or worry about our safety anywhere. Our children are kept in His hand. God does allow things to come into our lives that He might conform us to His image. What He allows, He will give sufficient grace for that trial. God has spoken and we will obey.

A LION'S SHARE

Despite the fact that the villagers worked from morning to night in their plantations, there were few amenities of life to show for it. This far off river village in the interior of the Likouala region was rich in pineapples and other garden delights that flourished in their area. If only someone would come to buy their produce, they would be able to go down river to the center, at Impfondo, and buy nice things for themselves and their children. The hopelessness of their plight led them to drink. They climbed the palm trees at dawn and dug holes in them to attach a gourd. Sweet palm juice would begin to drip into the container. Eventually, it fermented and became palm wine. When the sun set, the villagers sat and drank until they were drunk. Day after day, they opened the doors of their huts to repeat the same activity. They hoped that maybe some of their young people would score high enough on the government school exams so that they might leave this way of life and pursue jobs in the capital city.

The women bore the babies, worked the gardens, and cooked the evening meal. This would keep them for the next twenty-four hours. In between times, they might be able to find some papaya on a tree or some bananas. Thus, hunger was kept at a short distance until another night. These meager diets led to much malnutrition among the many children and elderly. Julienne and her mother, Rosine, arose early one day to make a tiresome trek to the jungle garden. Julienne was large with pregnancy and hoped that they might get home before nightfall. She longed for a satisfying meal and a good night's sleep. Every day she had told her husband that they needed something better in life. The two women arrived early at the garden and began to dig and hoe. The plantain cooking bananas had grown large. Carrying them home on her back would be a laborious job. She pushed the thought away as she dug.

Her selflessness must have driven her to dig one more hour. Before night fell, they loaded up their huge baskets that they would carry on their backs. The dry firewood would go in first and then the sweet potatoes, pineapples and bananas. Both women were suddenly startled. For a number of years, they had worked in the garden and arrived home safely. There was never any trouble with animals in the forest. This sound was different. In the quietness of their surroundings, the underbrush crackled. Before either one could grab a garden tool, an animal sprang into the air. He landed on one of the women and began a feast that was to consume his victims. It isn't known why the other didn't flee to the village, but the second would remain to die with the first. Night fell, Monkeys' screams broke the silence as they peered nervously at the beast. Now and then a night bird signaled the presence of an enemy.

Back in the village, the family wondered why Julienne and Rosine didn't come home. The husband of Julienne was quick to speak up and tell the villagers that if the women worked too late, they would stop at a hunter's encampment and sleep for the night. The hot, steamy day wore on and when the women didn't arrive the second night, the large extended family decided that they would leave early in the morning for the garden. Before starting out, they knocked on the door of Pastor Pierre. He warned the family to be cautious because the jungle was full of hazards. He assured them that he would be praying for them and hoped that Julienne hadn't given birth to her child way out there. The men stopped first at the hunter's camp and asked them if they had seen or heard the women. They told the husband that they had seen the women when they passed by the first day but that they had heard nothing more. Looking at one another, it was evident that they were very afraid. They all grasped their spears in a determined manner, not really knowing who the enemy was. After much walking they arrived at the garden.

There was no sign of life, just a deathly silence. Each one spread out a little to look behind each tree and bush. Suddenly, a family member called for a group to come to where he was standing. They hurried to the spot and looked on in terror. They wailed and wept. They threw their bodies to the ground. Blood was all over. No body parts were found, only the soles of their feet. What savage animal could have consumed so much? They couldn't imagine how any animal in this part of the forest could do such a thing. Only monkeys, leopards and gorillas roamed through this part of the jungle. Even a very hungry leopard would not do this. Had someone worked some witchcraft against the family or the village? They carefully put the soles of the women's feet in some banana leaves and carried them back to the village. Before they even arrived, they all began to wail and sing the songs of death. Villagers left their cooking and went out to meet them. The young men went to their huts and brought out the big drums. Evil had come to their midst and they must scare away the spirits that might come and carry some of them away. The hours dragged on. The fires were burning everywhere in the surroundings. Soon, the drum beating and wailing would begin again and the dancing would continue until morning.

Pasteur Pierre came into their midst and tried to console them with the Word of God. He reminded them that they had repeatedly spurned the voice of the Lord as He called them to turn to Him, to trust Him, to believe Him for Eternal Life. Sadly, they turned away and said that they would find the evil influences in their village who had done this.

Each day dawned and everyone was afraid to go to their jungle garden. When the sun set, they barred their fragile doors. Fear was so great that it could be felt from the oldest to the youngest. All feared that the evil spirits would come to carry them away.

One very late night when the moon was casting its shadow through the jungle trees, a low moan and growl could be heard. The sound echoed through the village and passed by every hut. Each family was huddling together.

This was not a sound that they had heard before. The sun shone brightly before the doors opened. Pastor Pierre gathered all the people together. His words were to shock everyone. He told the people that he spent a part of his growing up years in the Central African Republic, where he had been born. The sounds that he had heard in the night were comparable to the grunts and growls of a lion on the loose. The village chief was quick to remind him that lions were way to the north of them, perhaps a hundred miles away in the grasslands and the mountains. There could never be such an animal in their area. They must look for a way to make a trap to catch the large leopard, or so they thought.

One man stepped forward. Alexie was an enormous man of great height and strength. He was willing to go with his spear and machete to look for the leopard that had terrorized their little village. Nothing would be able to withstand him. He was wise in the ways of hunting and he wanted to show everyone that he was without fear.

Heavily armed, Alexie made his way down the jungle trail. He didn't go very far but far enough to entice the leopard. He waited and waited but saw nothing. He had forgotten to bring a bottle of water with him, so he took his round climbing apparatus and started up the palm tree. He spied a gourd and knew that after several days of no one taking down the gourds, there would be plenty of palm wine to drink. Time was on his hands. He drank and drank until he became happy. He had emptied the gourd and it was time to get back down on the ground. He was prepared to sit and wait several more hours before returning home. Somewhere in the underbrush, a very large animal was crouching waiting for the ideal moment to spring.

Alexie was careless and drunk. He no longer thought of the mission that he came on. Singing loudly and weaving from side to side, he trudged toward home. Big Alexie was now a picture of weakness and the crouching adversary knew it. The animal crept through the underbrush on its belly, waiting for the moment to spring on Alexie. He would have another free meal. Within sight of the village, the animal sprang into the air. The machete and the spear of Alexie fell to the ground. The animal leaped to the head and tore off his scalp. Hearing the screams of the dying man, the villagers grabbed pots and pans and began beating them. They saw the fallen Alexie on the path but they saw nothing else. Alexie screamed for them to kill him as his suffering was more than he could bear. He died in a pool of blood.

The evil spirits were surely unhappy with the villagers and it was time for them to do something about it. The notables gathered together and planned to make a trap that would catch this ferocious animal. Poles were cut to put in a square, much like a big room. They would put smaller poles together to form a wall and a trap door with a goat inside. When the animal heard the baaing of the goat, he would come. As the trap door fell on their enemy, they would all come and spear it. Victory was sure!

A large goat was chosen. This would surely entice the animal. Now, it was time to be patient and wait for his visit. He would not come to the village during the daylight hours. As night fell, the men were all together and talked in whispers. Would he come tonight? Would he take the bait that they had put in the cage? As the hours dragged on, they heard a low moan. The dogs cowered in the shadows of the small night lamps. This was surely their enemy. The silence was broken by the baa of the goat. He, too, sensed that something was seeking his life.

Without a sound, the animal stealthily crept ever closer to the caged goat. In a flash, he entered the cage and the trap door slammed down. The animal seemed to be caught. The villagers sprang from their huts and bounded toward the trap with eyes fixed on this beast. Before their eyes, they witnessed their enemy break the long, heavy sticks that made up the trap wall. He broke away with the goat in his mouth to the waiting night shadows. By this time, they had all retreated to the security of their mud huts. Breathlessly, they all began to whisper the word, "NKOSI" (lion). Words escaped them. They were not prepared to kill a lion of that size and power. They needed help in the way of a high powered rifle. The Chief spoke up and recalled that a Frenchman had passed by to hunt elephants to the north of them. They could send someone from their midst to call him.

Days passed by and the villagers became anxious. They couldn't go to their gardens, nor could they go hunt monkey or deer. Daylight fishing kept some food on their tables to ward off hunger. Early one morning, they heard the purr of an outboard motor. It had to be the Frenchman. The villagers ran down to the edge of the water to see who was approaching. Sure enough, it was the hunter. He got out of his boat and walked toward the meeting house where the whole village would sit and listen to his plan. The Chief recounted again the story down to every detail. The hunter asked them to make another cage that was very strong, one that a lion could not break. Close to the village, they began the task of cutting down sturdy trees that could not be broken by anything but an elephant. Everyone was aware that unless this savage beast was caught, they would all have to leave the home of their ancestors and they had no other home to go to. Since the lion had found a goat in the first cage, he would surely return again to the same spot when he was hungry. Younger men dug deep holes and put the sturdy trees in them.

They packed the earth around each tree to make sure that it would not bend over or come out. The goat was securely tied inside and the trap door was tried to make sure that it would spring down on the lion. The wait began and the Frenchman cleaned his big game rifle making sure that it would not miss fire. He paced nervously back and forth. Even with a rifle, he appeared fearful. They might sit all night waiting. There was always the possibility that the lion would go to another area of the jungles and another village.

They were all haunted by their thoughts because each man knew that they had to work their gardens if they were to eat. Some villagers grew weary waiting and returned to work their plantations. Without doubt the animal had gone somewhere else. Yet, in the days that followed, eleven more villagers failed to return home.

Certainly, all had met the same fate as Alexie. The Frenchman considered leaving. Hearing this, the Christians prayed that the lion would return. If the beast wasn't killed, they would all be eaten over a period of time.

One night as the moon went behind heavy cloud cover, the village was shrouded in mist and fog. All the dogs were cowering again in the corners of each hut. They all knew that the lion was moving through the village. The lion could surely smell the dogs, but he could also see the fat goat in the trap that had been built for him. The goat was agitated and his cries cut through the still, jungle night. All listened and waited for the trap to fall. Hearts were pounding as they peeked out their doors and waited for the Frenchman to yell out. The loud roar was suddenly heard as the trap door fell down behind the lion in the cage. Knowing that he was secured inside, they sprang from their hiding places. With night lanterns in hand, they ran to see the great capture. At last, they had their enemy! The Frenchman took aim with his high powered rifle and the huge beast fell down. He was dead at last, but at what cost? Twelve members of their village were now gone.

The lion was brought down to our center at Impfondo in a cage. It was a beautiful animal with an enormously long mane and a weight of five hundred pounds. It was surmised that the lion had entered the Congo from the Central African Republic when it was dry season. Lions are used to finding food in the grasslands and other open areas, not in jungles. Possibly, the rains came and the small streams became raging torrents. Caught on the Congo side, he found the easiest prey available – man. I could not help but think of what God says in His Word concerning the lion. In I Peter 5:8 we have a very sobering picture of our own adversary who also seeks to destroy us. "Be sober, be vigilant: because your adversary the devil, as a roaring lion, walketh about, seeking whom he may devour."

All who were killed by this animal did not know the Lord. They had resisted the messages that Pastor Pierre preached each Sunday. They had waited for a more convenient day and that day never came. Each one had hoped to see a new day but their life was cut short and all went to meet God as a judge and not as a Savior. Our life on this earth is so very short. We must walk soberly before our Heavenly Father and be ever mindful of His promise to us. "And when the chief Shepherd shall appear, ye shall receive a crown of glory that fadeth not away (I Peter 5:4).

The sinking boat in the jungle waters

THE SINKING BOAT
IN JUNGLE WATERS

Missionary wives are a breed of their own. It was understood when we volunteered for God's service in Africa that we were going to risk our lives many times in our efforts to preach the Gospel in every village that was hidden in the dense forest. Dangers were real. Many Africans in our large region had encountered accidents of many kinds. Storms had caused their boats to sink in the rivers. Wild animal encounters had taken the lives of countless others as they crisscrossed thousands of square miles of jungle. Listening to the stories of life in this forgotten area gave us an insight into our future life.

Gene had done river work along the narrow, winding waterways from the first year that we had arrived in northern Congo. Sometimes, I went with him but as the children were yet small, I stayed home to care for them. Later on when they were at mission school or in America, I traveled more extensively. Thousands of sick people lived in that forest and few had any medical care. Using my medical skills was a way of showing Christ's love and a way into their hearts. Jesus often healed the sick and then He preached the Kingdom of Heaven. People listened to His message when they were whole and became His followers. We found this to be true also.

Gene began to make plans to carry the Word of God to the backcountry. Many lived in those areas and died alone in their jungle villages. A great number had never gone out to see the outside world. Although I was often frightened when meandering along the snake like waterways deep in the forest, I never told anyone that I could not swim. At least I thought that I couldn't. When my husband asked me to go with him, I thought about it a long time and then decided to stay at the mission station and take care of the hundreds of people who were coming to the dispensary each week. The needs were as great on the station as they were in the jungle villages.

After his departure, I wondered if I had done the right thing. All of these random thoughts were quickly forgotten as I worked twelve hours at the dispensary and then checked on leprosy patients at the main hospital. From time to time, people would come by dugout from the forest villages and they would tell me in which village they had seen the pastor. Many were coming to Christ and churches were being established. The responsibilities were many as we contemplated the number of Bible school graduates that would serve in various areas. They would each be responsible for a number of smaller villages that were close to their home base. This would mean much traveling for them as well. Small outboard motors were needed to help them go farther. Paddling down swift jungle waterways was easy but returning against the current consumed a great deal of energy.

Several weeks passed by and I had heard no recent word from Gene. Was he ill with malaria, was his heart giving him problems and how were his supplies lasting? We had no way to communicate except for an occasional fisherman or hunter who would take a letter in the hopes that they would come across my husband. They say that no news is good news, but in this case, that was of little comfort. The more I prayed, the more I felt that something had gone terribly wrong. Lifting him and the pastors with him before the Throne of grace was engulfing my every thought. One evening, quite late, a man knocked at my door. I was alone on the station except for the night guard. He spoke in a very concerned voice as he said, "I heard from some villagers that the pastor's boat had sunk."

Sheer terror grabbed at my heart. I was upset with the man that he had no other information. Why didn't he ask some questions? Was he okay? Did someone go to his rescue? That night was very long as I struggled to sleep. Not having a shred of news was simply awful. I needed some assurances from God that all was well. As the days turned into another, no news arrived. I earnestly prayed for peace. Not knowing the outcome of his accident was tearing me apart inside. Opening God's Word for answers, a portion of Romans 5:1-5 seemed to jump out at me. "Therefore being justified by faith, we have peace through our Lord Jesus Christ: By whom also we have access by faith into this grace wherein we stand, and rejoice in hope of the glory of God. And not only so, but we glory in tribulation also; knowing that tribulation worketh patience, and patience, experience, and experience, hope: And hope maketh not ashamed; because the love of God is shed abroad in our hearts by the Holy Spirit which is given unto us."

This was God's Word for me. No matter what came to pass, God would watch over us in all circumstances and His will would be done. My hope now was in God's provision. All of these experiences were used to mold me into the vessel that He could use. We are to be conformed to His image and often the whittling processes of God bring about real pain. We aren't always submissive to His will. We do not think it is fair when we pass through such deep trials and hurt. Yet, He waits for us to flee into His arms that we might feel His love, that we might know that He will give us the Grace to pass through the fiery trials of life.

As the sun was setting beyond the jungle wall, God ministered to my heart. In the distance, I heard loud voices, some were shouting. I couldn't hear what was going on so I ran outside and over to the edge of the river. Gene and all the Congolese pastors, who had traveled with him, were getting out of the dugout. There was an overwhelming relief that poured over me. It was like a refreshing rain. My dear husband was bolting up the embankment to gather me into his arms. He was safe! God was faithful in caring for him. After all the equipment in the dugout had been taken out and carried to the storehouse, it was time to hear his story.

Their journey had gone well and they had preached in every village. Many were accepting Christ as Savior and the Congolese pastors and some of the Bible school students were filled with a desire to serve God and to disciple this hidden group of people, including thousands and thousands of Pygmies. As they made their way down stream through the deep forest, they found many fallen trees. Storms and high winds had broken off huge branches of trees that rose a hundred and fifty feet into the air. Sometimes, they noticed that fishermen had cut the trees to make the narrow waterway more passable and other times the tree was poorly cut and a part of it could be seen barely under the water. Suddenly and without warning, the thirty-foot dugout rose up as if a huge hand had lifted it. As it quickly settled, water began pouring into the boat. The men were so frightened that they all moved to one side to straighten the dugout. Without thinking, they jumped out of the boat. Gene was left with the handle of the five horse Evinrude in his hand. A big wave moved to where he was sitting on the edge of the boat and he knew that the boat was sinking. He, too, jumped out and swam toward a tree that was grounded in deep water. They looked at one another in exasperation and disbelief. How could this possibly happen to them when they were miles from the next village. They watched as a very poisonous snake swam by. Each one knew that crocodiles were everywhere in the black water. Soon, it would be night and there was no shelter, no safety.

Gene made a decision that would save their lives. He would strip down and dive down in the sixteen feet of water and see where the boat was. Putting his watch on some twigs in the tree branches, he went down, down, down and there it was! The boat was sitting, stuck in the mud on the bottom. They had to do something to get it out. He pushed his way to the surface where the others were anxiously waiting for him to pop out of the water. They all agreed to go down and pull up on the boat to free it from the mud. With a shout of sheer energy they broke through the water and tipped it slightly to push out the water inside. The empty gasoline barrels had to be retrieved from the high weeds beside the larger trees. The full barrel of gasoline was to give them a great deal of grief as they tried over and over to get it into the boat. With no land anywhere, it seemed an impossible situation. After the water had been scooped out of the boat, they all sat on the edge of the boat hanging onto the trees. They lifted their voices in prayer, asking God to help them get the heavy gasoline barrels into the dugout. Some were in the boat, others were treading water. With a one, two and three, they heaved hard and the barrels were pushed up and into the boat. They all sensed that it wasn't their strength that had done the job. The very hand of God had done it. They had prayed, they had believed and God did the rest.

It was time to survey the situation and make a quick inventory of what had been lost. The barrels of bedding and mosquito nets would surely be safe and dry because the barrel had a very tight lid on it. The gifts of chicken from the villagers had drowned and one plastic sandal had disappeared. Everything else seemed to be okay. It all came up just as it had sunk. Much time was used up in cleaning the water from the carburetor of the outboard motor. Night began to fall as they finished the task of fixing the motor. They pulled the rope and the motor sprang to life. Very carefully, Gene guided the motor around the dangerous curves and all watched for underwater logs. They did not wish to repeat the same drama as before. The darkness was casting shadows. After hitting a tree head-on, they knew it was time to shut off the motor and continue down river by paddle. In the stillness of the approaching night, crocs could be heard bellowing. They were all chilled from being wet. They were also very hungry as they hadn't eaten all day. Night had come to the forest and the small flashlights that they retrieved from a footlocker soon gave out.

With absolutely no light of any kind, they swished their paddles slightly in an effort to keep the boat in the narrow waterway. Some wanted to tie up to a tree. Others wanted to keep going, be it ever so slowly. The mosquitoes came out in full force and they felt that they were being eaten alive. As the boat floated on in silence, they all were aware that no village was nearby. Only God knew of their plight and it seemed that they had no options. The still, black night brought forth unusual noises. Fear was creeping in and a feeling of utter helplessness.

A sound penetrated the darkness that was like no other. It sounded like people. They listened. There was hope. Then it was still again. They continued to drift. There it was. Voices could be heard. There was no village nearby. Who were they and where were they? They all decided to yell at once and call for help. With united shouts, they called. In the distance, they heard a reply. Their boat had drifted near a small parcel of higher ground that was a fishing encampment. They would have a place to sleep. God had provided a place of safety, a refuge.

One barrel was taken from the dugout. It had the bedding and the sponge mattresses inside. Near the fire that the fishermen had made, they opened the barrel to get their supplies. The day had been too long and they were weary to the bone. As the barrel was opened, they gazed inside. Everything was completely soaked. The barrel was old and there were, without doubt, small pinpoint holes that allowed water to enter. Gene felt so weary that he didn't care. He felt sure that he could sleep on anything but having wet clothes and sleeping in wet sheets wasn't going to work. He tossed and turned way into the night and finally joined all the rest of his crew around the hot, open fire. They sat there until dawn. Having brought rope with them, they stretched it out between trees so that they could put the sponge mattresses and sheets up to dry. They would have to stay there the better part of the day to make sure that their sleeping gear was dry.

They looked at the supplies. At least they would have rice to eat. The rice was all wet, too, and it wouldn't take long for that to rot in the heat and dampness. At this point, they had completed half of their planned evangelism trip. Some brought up the subject of returning home. After all, new food supplies would have to be obtained somewhere and it seemed that they had suffered enough. After emptying their hearts of what was vexing them, they had a long prayer meeting. God brought to their minds that many in the remaining villages had not heard the message of Salvation. Would they turn back now just when they were on the threshold of bringing Eternal Hope to those lost in heathen darkness? It was settled. All agreed that they could not turn their back on the opportunities that God had given them. Although they had suffered, they would continue. Gene and the group of national pastors could not go home.

Because of their faithfulness, God abundantly blessed the preaching of the Word in each village and many more were added to the church of Jesus Christ. They went forth by faith, trusting their Heavenly Father that He would accomplish His perfect will through them. In good and bad times, they pressed on. There was another man, a long time ago, whose name was Abraham. He knew what it was like to go forward in the face of uncertainty. The Bible says, "By faith, Abraham, when he was called to go out into a place which he should after receive for an inheritance, obeyed; and he went out, not knowing whither he went. By faith he sojourned in the land of promise, as in a strange country, dwelling in tabernacles with Isaac and Jacob, the heirs with him of the same promise: For he looked for a city which hath foundations, whose builder and maker is God" (Hebrews 11:8-10). We, too, had gone, by faith, to a country we had not seen before. Because of a host of believers who prayed and held us up before God each day, we would be able to enter into the inheritance, someday, that God had reserved for His own.

By faith, many more will start out on that journey to continue the task of those who went before. Some will give their lives. Some will be persecuted, tortured and mistreated for Jesus' sake, but all will enter into the reward that God has promised to all those who are steadfast and faithful to Him.

HIJACKED ON FLIGHT 102

It was a hot, sticky night when the 727 took off from the Abidjan airport in Ivory Coast West Africa. It was vacation time and our daughter, Patricia, was returning home to the Congo. She attended the Conservative Baptist high school in Northern Ivory Coast and looked forward to the breaks at Christmas time and the end of the school period in June. The plane was scheduled to touch down in the Republic of Gabon, take on more passengers and continue on to Brazzaville where her father would be waiting for her.

The flight was ordinary and the weather cooperated to give them a nice, smooth flight. She got some of her things together so that there would be less to take care of at the last minute when they gave cards to fill out. In African countries, there are always so many papers to fill out about every aspect of a person's life. We could never really appreciate the fact that we could drive from New York to California without stopping every few miles for identity checks, that is until we lived in Africa. At every turn, one was asked for a passport or identity card, where one lives, what one is doing and where one is going. Nothing escapes the ever piercing eyes of each government on the African continent.

Behind Patricia's seat, there seemed to be some commotion. She then heard a woman begin to scream. An

African was standing in the aisle with a machete knife in his hand. He was holding a large sharpened machete to the throat of a woman. He evidently had tied the long knife around his inner leg and then took it out at the appropriate time. Security wasn't all that tight in that country. The man began to scream some orders and those orders were to be taken to the pilots of the Air Africa plane. He threatened to knock out all the windows and kill everyone if his demands were not met. As everyone was yelling, screaming and crying, the situation became almost unbearable on board.

Patricia said that she, too, was crying loudly. She was close to arrival in Brazzaville and now she was going to die. As she sobbed, God brought to her a panoramic view of her whole life. She pondered her unusual and prema-ture birth and how she wasn't supposed to live. Yet, God saved her life because He had purpose for her. He had kept her and brought her to this moment in time. Surely, her life couldn't end now. She took note of her surround-ings and stopped crying. It was time to pray about this terrible situation. Surely, God was able to intervene again in her life. She prayed for the pilots that God would give them wisdom in how to deal with this man who seemed totally unstable, mixed up and almost crazy. The captain was called and he began to question the crazed passenger. The young fellow, of about twenty-four years of age, wanted to return to the Ivory Coast and if his wishes were not met, he would surely kill everyone aboard.

Since they were cruising about 35,000 feet, this could take place in a very short time. The pilot, unknown to the madman, was stalling for time and finally told him they did not have sufficient fuel to be able to return to Ivory Coast. The pilot formed a plan to trick the man by telling him that they would return. The plane made an abrupt circle and turned north. It was true that fuel was not sufficient to return to Ivory Coast, but it could take them to the Republic of Gabon, a stop they had just made. As the man stood facing all the passengers, the pilot quietly spoke by radio to the control tower in Gabon. The police were asked to be on hand when the doors sprang open.

Patricia sat stunned, thinking that this was like a scene from a television program. Knowing that God was with her, she felt comforted. He was standing right beside her. Meanwhile, Patricia's father was waiting in Brazzaville for the 10 pm flight to come in. Each hour dragged by. Finally, the loud speaker crackled and a policeman informed the people that they had received news of a hijacking for her flight. Gene returned to his room where he was staying with Mr. John Ruffner, an African American who worked for the American Embassy. He was troubled at hearing the news but more for the small amount of information that was offered. There was cause for alarm and a need for much prayer. Having been told that the plane would probably arrive the next morning, he went to bed and fell into a troubled sleep. In the middle of the night, the beeper went off in the bedroom of John Ruffner. A marine at the American Embassy was calling for Pastor Thomas.

The message was given and Gene awoke hearing an urgent knock on his bedroom door. He was told to go immediately to the Embassy. It was 3:00 am on July 2, 1985. Gene borrowed John's jeep and hurried through the empty streets of the capital. Arriving at the beautifully lit embassy, he identified himself to the guards and rushed to the front door of the building. Patricia was there waiting for her father.

The police had grabbed the emotionally disturbed man at the Gabon Airport and took him away. After refueling, the plane continued on to Brazzaville. Patricia went through customs, got her baggage and a taxi and proceeded to the Embassy. We had gone through this scenario many, many times with her but never really believing that it would ever happen. As she ran into her father's arms, the tears were released. The day had been way too long and too full of horrifying experiences. Her emotions gave way to relief and happiness to be safe.

Back at the jungle outpost of Impfondo, some 650 miles away, I had no idea of what had transpired. Only when they flew north and arrived safely home did I learn of all the details of this terrifying trip.

It reinforced our feelings of fear when sending her so far away to school. But, there was no other way to go. Another Christian school was available in Kenya but it would mean getting on three planes to get there and this was not an option for us. If one plane wasn't flying due to repairs or weather, she could be left in some strange village without any help and no way of communication.

In every situation, prayer was needed as we watched our children go away to school. There were numerous times when we were on planes that had mechanical problems, but God kept us safe and brought us to our destination. Yet, we have to be candid when we say that we never felt completely comfortable when flying around Africa as we knew that the planes were not maintained in a proper way. There were many accidents that took the lives of people over the years that we lived there. Each time we flew, we would bow and commit our ways and our children to our Heavenly Father. By day and by night, He does guard those who belong to Him. God never allows anything to befall us that isn't in His perfect will.

How can we know that He is watching over us personally? Matthew 10:29-31 tells us, "Are not two sparrows sold for a farthing? And one of them shall not fall on the ground without your Father knowing? But the very hairs of your head are all numbered. Fear ye not therefore, ye are of more value than many sparrows."

CATHERINE,
FLOWER FROM DRY GROUND

We were aghast as we saw first hand the deep needs of those people who were living in dire circumstances, poverty and diseases. At that time, we didn't realize that Catherine was among those who were listening to the Gospel story for the first time. As we sat on some little stools outside by a fire that held a large cooking pot, Catherine began to pour out her story. She remembered: "The sky was blue, but I didn't see it. Flowers bloomed but I never smelled their scent. I was a child, but knew not the joys that belonged to a vibrant childhood. Many people in my far off and isolated jungle village were sad. So many were ill and had bad smelling sores. The once lovely faces, that I loved, changed and contorted as their illness progressed. I looked at my own frail body and noticed changes taking place. I couldn't understand what was happening to the others, or me, that I saw sitting daily before their huts."

Leprosy hospital dedication plaque

"One day, some French men came and they lined us up and began to look at and examine our bodies. Bodies

171

that were once strong had turned into festering sores. Hands and feet became gnarled and ugly. They told us that we had a sickness called leprosy. They said that they would have to make a village especially for all those who had this dreaded disease. I was growing into a young woman and no one wanted me to be their wife. I would never know the thrill of a suckling child at my breasts and a

home filled with the sounds of excited children. For me, the birds would never sing again. Darkness surrounded me and I was imprisoned and lonely."

Leprosy in the legs

"Late one hot afternoon, we all heard an outboard motor. We all limped slowly down to the edge of the river. A missionary couple got out of the dugout canoe and said that they had good news for everyone. They wanted us to come to some meetings each morning and evening."

"They brought along a Congolese pastor who would remain behind and tell us more from a book called the Bible. A Pastor Thomas spoke about Jesus. Who was this Jesus? I hadn't heard about Him before. What could He do for me? Within my heart, I felt a tug and was compelled to go to every service and listen to words from the black book. The missionary said that this Jesus came to earth long ago to save people from their sins and whosoever believed in Him would receive life everlasting. He told us that Jesus was killed by evil men but that Jesus arose again that I might live. Much time passed. Little by little, I was losing my fingers and toes. My heart longed to have that new body that the pastor preached about. Was there no hope for me? A year went by and my soul yearned for love and companionship. The African pastor told me that if all others forsook me, Jesus would love me and stand by me. That day, I turned my ugly and broken body over to Him. I also gave Him my heart that I might serve Him."

"The bitterness is gone now and I can laugh again. My fingers and toes are also gone, but I have the hope of a

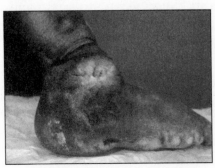

new body someday. I can now look up to the blue sky and know that sometime in the future, Jesus will descend to take me unto Himself. Though my earthly house is undesirable and unlovely, my heart is not damaged or

Leprous foot that Sandy amputated

marred. It hears a new and heavenly song."

"My face is ugly, but I look up to behold the beauty of my Savior. I have nothing left to give Him in this world, but a heart of gratitude and praise. I kneel before Him. I adore Him. Because He lives, I, too, shall live. I await His coming to transform this broken bit of clay into a beautiful vessel. I will love and serve Him until that day in the future when He calls my name. I will then step over the Jordan into His beauty and Glory. I have never been able to sing, but then I will join the Heavenly choir as it sings Majesty to the King. I will be numbered in their midst forever."

God uses the disease of leprosy to show what our sins look like before Him. Isaiah 1:18 tells us, "Come now, and let us reason together, saith the Lord: though your sins be as scarlet, they shall be as white as the snow; though they be red like crimson, they shall be as wool." This day, we can be clean and pure before our Lord if we confess our sins that are destroying us without and within. He, the Lord, will cleanse us and wash away all our sins. Now is the day of Salvation to all who will believe and trust in the Lord Jesus as Savior.

Leprosy, or Hanson's disease, has been a problem in the northern part of Congo for a long time. When the French Colonists were in charge, they had leprosy colonies in the jungle where they endeavored to treat all the lepers in one place. As the years went by, better medicine was found to treat the disease and they allowed the people to leave and live with their own families.

A number of years ago, my husband took an old building at the central hospital and with aid from the American Embassy and other European Embassies, rebuilt the building to house a few men and women who needed constant care. There was also a treatment and operating room. Much financial help was given to make this small facility a reality where lepers in the whole area could come each week to have their sores bandaged and to receive their weekly pills. They were treated for malaria, parasites and other illnesses as well.

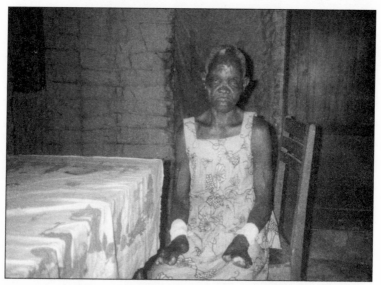

This is Catherine, she is now with the Lord.

This facility continues to bring hope to ill lepers and house those who are from far away areas. The American Leprosy Foundation has had a great part in supplying our vehicles and meds that we might bring hope to those who are in dire circumstances.

Some of the lepers were vibrant Christians who brought a lot of joy to us as we worked with them. One of these was Catherine, a lady who had lost most of her fingers and toes. My heart was always touched each Sunday morning as Catherine limped to the front of the church and placed her offering in the plate. Over her hands was a hankie to cover the stubs that remained for fingers. In the palm of the two joined hands was her offering to Jesus, a very precious gift to our Lord.

I visited Catherine one afternoon to listen to her story of how she came to the Savior. I was carried back to former years when we first visited her village. I was a young woman and very impressionable as we visited the many jungle villages along the Libenga River.

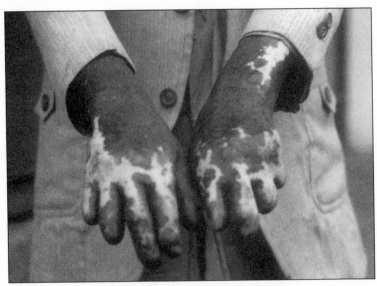

The effects of leprosy on a man's hands

WILLEY'S LEGACY

Our hearts were full and running over as God opened up new ministries. There was so much to keep us occupied. With the literacy program, the Bible school classes, children's work, river evangelization, church planting and women's work, we felt fulfilled. Yet, in the back of our minds, we knew that there should be a medical work. The jungle people had many diseases. As we traveled the winding rivers of the interior, our hearts became burdened to ease the suffering of those with major and minor diseases. I say minor because they seemed that way in light of the debilitating illnesses such as yaws, tuberculosis, sleeping sickness and leprosy.

When we were yet in Bible College, I was interested in becoming a doctor or nurse. Much to our surprise, young married women could not be in a medical program when married, unless they were willing to live apart from their partners and enter under their maiden name. In the depths of my heart, the desire to work with sick people never left me. Somehow, I felt that God would work out His perfect plan and give me the desires of my heart.

The local hospital had a nursing program that was under the direction of the National Red Cross. When a local Congolese Administrator saw that I was giving medical help to villagers, he suggested that I take the nursing course that was being offered in French. I jumped at the chance as this would be the fulfillment of a hidden dream. Nursing in this part of Africa is different than in the United States. It offered more opportunities to have hands on with patients. Laboratory work was part of the program to study the various parasites that were in our area, take blood samples for sickle cell anemia, leprosy smears and many other diseases. The lab work fascinated me, but the Lord never wanted me to become involved in this full time. Looking into the microscope hour after hour caused me to have severe headaches. Having mastered what I needed to know for a future medical ministry, I left that to work in surgery for two years.

My talent immediately surfaced and I had a great eagerness to learn all there was to know about suturing cuts from axes, machetes and other work related accidents. It wasn't unusual for hunters to come who had been bitten by monkeys that they tried to pick up before the animal was dead. A few had been gored by buffalo and wild pig. Opportunities were many, day and night. My heart longed to give that added labor of love to parents whose children were burning up with malaria.

My husband built our first cement medical building and it was dedicated in 1966 to serve the jungle people. We never could have imagined that thousands upon thousands would pass through those doors over the next three decades. It was an oasis for needy people, a refuge for the old and a place for renewed life that was offered to the little children. Many books could be written to tell the stories of the families and individuals who came for help. They received more than just medicine. They got tracts and a message that pointed them to the Great Physician who could give them true Life in Christ. Students and pastors took turns reading from the Word and praying for all who came. Witch doctors, Muslims from West

Africa and African cult people came. They were sent away with more than what they came for. The Word that was planted in their hearts made them responsible to accept or reject the love of Jesus that was manifest to them there.

After returning home from the hospital, I found my husband tired and exhausted after battling with tire troubles for a wagon that would be used with the tractor. There were so many frustrations since we couldn't go to a store and buy the parts, tools and pieces that we needed. In the U.S., no one thinks twice about running over to the store for whatever is needed. Being creative was certainly an asset in this far off corner of the world. After tirelessly pursuing the job at hand, he came in to eat lunch and take a needed siesta.

No sooner had we sat down to lunch when anxious voices were heard on the patio. Answering the persistent knock, we were given a letter sent to us from a missionary in the Democratic Republic of the Congo. He was with Wycliffe Translators and was working on the Ubangui River, a few hours upriver by speedboat. The missionary had paid for gas so that a local villager could bring a young man to us by outboard motor. At our feet was a mat all rolled up with something inside. We were perplexed as we looked at the thin roll. Several people unrolled the mat and there lay a young lad in the most pitiful condition that we had ever seen, and believe me, we had seen some very bad cases over the years.

A few months before, while working hard in his mother's plantation, he became ill with fever. Other complications soon followed. It seemed evident, according to their description of his illness, that he may have had polio. Because his father had just drowned in a dugout canoe accident, the mother was left penniless. There was no money to go to a medical facility to treat her son. Left with no care, he finally became paralyzed from the waist down. No one in the village had any serious thought of helping the mother to send out the young man to a hospital. Week after week, he lay in his bed while his mother tried desperately to help him in every way possible. Soon, bad bedsores broke out on his frail body, a body that was once so strong and healthy.

Six months passed by before the young lad's physical condition worsened. He was then carried to the Wycliffe missionary. As I assessed his condition, I realized there was no hope for him. The femur bone on each leg was exposed at least twelve inches up and down the leg. The tendons were eaten away and the bones had already separated. The mother had no money to buy dressings, so old dirty rags had been tied around his body to keep in the body fluids and to keep out the flies. The infection was slowly eating up the buttocks. God was merciful in that He allowed him to be paralyzed so that he would not feel the terrible pain that he would ordinarily have suffered.

I asked him, "Nkombo na yo ejali nini?" (What is your name?)

He replied, "Nkombo na ngai ejali Willey." (My name is Willey)

In his hand, he was clutching something. He was quick to ask me, "Do you have to take my book away from me?"

I answered that I didn't but asked what was the book?

"It is my Bible, Mondele, (white person), and it is the only thing in life that I own," he said.

It was evident that Willey had a special relationship with God. He knew how to talk with God and he was holding on to God's promises that no matter what happened from this time forward, he would never be alone. His big dark eyes so filled with suffering, studied my face in an effort to find a ray of hope for him and his mother.

People came and went as they looked at this pitiful

piece of body that probably didn't weigh any more than forty pounds. Willey was fifteen years old, but he had been reduced to nothing but rotting flesh. After several hours of washing Willey's sores and putting on dressings, we sat and had prayer with him. Some who were standing by watching this scene unfold, walked away to the grass where they gave up their last meal.

We asked the mother if they had any relatives in the next village. Since the people on our side of the river and the villagers on the other side intermarried, it was not strange that the lady had some close or distant relatives in the area. Gene carefully laid Willey in the back of the pickup truck and took him and the mother to Bakandi, which was a village, more or less, for foreigners. We asked the direction to the homes of her family and they directed us to the house.

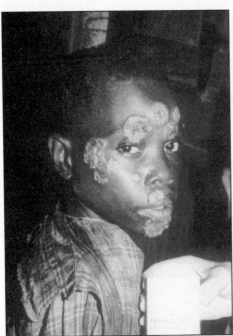

A village boy with Yaws disease

There was one small mud hut, about nine by nine feet, that was used for storage. There happened to be a bed inside made of wood and raffia. It was a very uncomfortable looking bed and one that I would never desire to sleep on. The room was dark, dirty and dank. A small lantern had to be lit so that we could see to work on Willey's sores when we made our daily visits. Gene left us while we were trying to make Willey comfortable. He sought out the Congolese doctor who was at the hospital nearby. As the doctor left the hut, the tears were streaming down his cheeks. The situation was critical and very sad. The doctor realized that there was nothing that anyone could do and said that perhaps Mrs. Thomas should care for him at least until he passed away.

Every day, when my long hours of work were over at the dispensary, I got into the Land Rover and made my way through the deep mud holes that made up the Bakandi streets. It was often 10 p.m. at night when I arrived at the hut. Always, Willey said that he was lending an ear to listen for my Land Rover to turn down the street. It was the highlight in his day. A young Congolese pastor began going with me to read the Bible to Willey and to sing him a song. He looked forward to this time and the fellowship that we offered. Few ever entered the hut because of the putrid smell that came from Willey's sores, so he spent a lot of long and lonely days. During each visit, Willey held his Bible, a treasure that surpassed all things in this life.

Realizing that Willey's fever was mounting a little

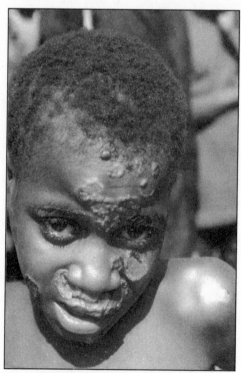

A Pygmie boy with yaws disease

each day, I knew that it wouldn't be long until he went on to meet the Lord. On a Friday evening, I had a special prayer for him. Then I explained that his body was decaying and Jesus would soon come into his room and carry him to Heaven. His face lit up as I explained that his suffering would soon be over and he would have a new body. His legs would work again and he would walk the streets of gold. All this awaited him because he was a child of the King of Kings.

The next day was a Saturday. The sun was shining brightly when I walked out of the house to get into the Land rover. I reopened the door and went back inside to get a white sheet and some money. God spoke to my heart and let me know that that day Willey would enter His Presence.

I arrived at the hut. It was still inside. I called Willey and he answered in a very weak voice. The family brought the little lantern so that I could see. I cut away the bandages that were soaked with body fluids. The smells were difficult to take, but God gives special grace during those times to do what must be done. Willey's breathing was coming in gasps and I noticed that he didn't open his eyes to talk with me. The time was at hand. I prayed again with him and committed him to our wonderful Lord. I took the stethoscope and listened to his heart. It was racing so much that he was panting. He had a difficult time to catch each breath after that. As I dressed his deep sores, I knew that I was preparing him for his burial. Willey's life was fading away, much like a mist. I had been with him two hours and near the end, the grandmother entered the hut and asked if she could help. I said that it would be nice of her if she would turn his body as I wrapped him in large bandages that I had received from the many women missionary societies.

As we walked out of the mud hut into the sunshine

once more, the grandmother looked at me a long time and said, "White lady, nobody, but nobody but one of God's people, could do what you have done. I want to know the God that you serve."

Because of the service of love that I had rendered in the name of the Lord, a whole family came to Christ. I gave the mother some money to buy rice and coffee. Just as I was leaving, the Grandmother asked me to return to the room where Willey lay. I entered. All was still. I listened to his heart and I smiled. Jesus had visited that humble place and took Willey across the Jordan. In his hand, he still clutched the little black New Testament. He would be buried just like that.

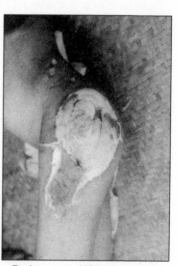

Bedsores on Willey's buttock

While riding back to the Mission station, I could hear the call that we had received so long ago. We had been commissioned to carry the Gospel, no matter what the cost might be. We had been sent to give hope to those in a needy land. This was only one facet of that ministry. The tears were hot as they streamed down my face. There were times when I had felt sorry for myself because of the hardships that we had to face. Yet, young Willey had endured a suffering that I probably would never have to endure, and he had never once uttered one word of complaint.

We had been sent to minister and give a cup of cold water in His Name. If life had dealt us some hard blows, if we had suffered, if we had cried and walked through some dark valleys, we had never walked alone. Our Heavenly Father was walking with us each step of the way. Although

I had fostered some ideas of giving up and going home, Willey's life had challenged me to continue on until my work on earth was done. Willey had won more people to Christ in his fifteen years on this earth than most people win in a lifetime. We had truly been challenged to be good soldiers of the Cross, to face the enemy and become victors in the battle that we would yet face.

Willey never made a great name for himself. He never came into fame, but because of his steadfastness for Christ, his whole household came to know the Lord. His legacy would live on forever.

My husband and I determined to walk a little closer to God and to hold the Word dearer to our hearts that we might be more productive in our corner of the world. Someday, our work for our Heavenly Father will be scrutinized and the rewards will be given to those who are faithful. He will separate those who served Him in love and those who gave only works for their own praise.

"When the Son of Man shall come in His glory, and all the holy angels with Him, then shall He sit upon the throne of His glory. And before Him shall be gathered all nations: and He shall separate them one from another, as a shepherd divideth His sheep from the goats: And He shall set the sheep on His right hand, but the goats on the left.

Then shall the King say unto them on His right hand, Come, ye blessed of my Father, inherit the kingdom prepared for you from the foundation of the world: For I was an hungered, and ye gave me meat: I was thirsty, and ye gave me drink: I was a stranger, and ye took me in: Naked, and ye clothed me: I was sick, and ye visited me: I was in prison, and ye came unto me.

And the king shall answer and say unto them, Verily I say unto you, Inasmuch as ye have done it unto one of the least of these my brethren, ye have done it unto me" (Matthew 25:31-36, 40). God is calling us today to serve

Him in gladness of heart. In some small way, we will bear fruit for Him and that fruit we shall lay at His feet when we stand in His Presence.

CHRIST VERSUS COMMUNISM

The Congo was going through a great deal of turbulence during the '70s. They were not sure if they wanted to be a little more moderate or become a part of the more popular movement of Maoism and Russian Communism. They began to shift from Scientific Socialism to full fledged Communism that controlled each citizen each day and made every decision from birth to grave.

The churches in the Congo were greatly affected by these sudden decisions. The government started some plantations but often took over the private plantations of those who had lucrative areas of coffee and cocoa beans. Every Saturday, the churches were forced to go to the government gardens and cut down the weeds and carry out the debris dumped on them from high winds and fallen trees. No one dared to stand up and refuse the orders of the government.

In 1975, 25 church organizations were asked to leave the country. Our own national church association was seeking autonomy and we saw problems on the horizon. During a six month period of that year, the local government closed down all our churches and every activity of the church was to cease. Being home on furlough at this particular time, we were following the situation with heavy hearts. We were about two months from returning to the Congo. Something seemed very strange to us. We had applied for our visas from the Congolese Embassy in Washington and they had sent them back to us allowing us to work for another three years. How could it be that we were being given permission to work when they had closed the work down?

Upon our return, my husband, Gene, and Pastor Mowawa, the national church president, made plans to go down to the capital to see the President of the country. It was absolutely necessary to open the doors of all the churches if we were to do a work for the Lord during our term of service. Otherwise, there was no need to remain in the country.

A dark secret began emerging. The local military commander of our region was looking for a nice place to house all the high brass of the area. What better way to take care of them than to house them in the missionary homes on the mission station. By doing this, they would not have to build anything and they would have an immediate place that was clean and beautiful. It would be

Pointing to the board that was nailed to keep the church doors shut

easy to tell the government in the South that the religious work at Impfondo was a sect and that would call for an expulsion of the missionaries who were working there. It would also do away with the Impfondo church and all the buildings and these could be used for meetings and a dance hall as well as drinking bars. This had been done with missionary property to the southeast of Impfondo and they were hoping to duplicate the same procedure in this area.

Mr. Batea, the area commander, had not reckoned with God. Gene and Pastor Mowawa talked with all seven men who surrounded the President when they went to Brazzaville. It was God's timing because all seven men were from our area of the Likouala Region. My husband told them how every church in the area had been barred, the monies from the churches had been confiscated and some of the church furnishings had been stolen by the military. The President's counsel became angry and they were mystified. They had not received any letters about the situation and most of all, they had not been told of any decision to expel the missionaries. How could this happen? The men told my husband and Pastor Mowawa to return

The government ordered that our church doors be opened

home and they would look into this serious matter.

When the men came home to Impfondo, the commander warned them that they were not to mention anything to anyone lest something awful befall them. This was a threat that meant danger could befall any of us. Gathering the local pastors together, we prayed. It was now or never. We would face this wicked man and the whole government, pray and let God do the work.

If we were to remain, we had to have a measure of freedom and the churches had to be reopened. We opened the Scriptures and looked to God for an answer. Surely, God would intervene for us and spare His Church in this dark hour. God led us to the story of Jehoshaphat and how God defeated Moab and Ammon. We read in II Chronicles 20:5-12:

> "And Jehoshaphat stood in the congregation of Judah and Jerusalem, in the house of the Lord, before the new court, and said, 'O Lord God of our fathers, art not thou God in heaven? And rulest not thou over all the kingdoms of the heathen? And in Thine hand is there not power and might, so that none is able to withstand thee? Art not thou our God, who didst drive out the inhabitants of this land before thy people Israel, and gavest it to the seed of Abraham thy friend forever? And they dwelt therein, and have built thee a sanctuary therein for thy name, saying, If, when evil cometh upon us, as the sword, judgment, or pestilence, or famine, we stand before this house, and in thy presence, (for thy name is in this house,) and cry unto thee in our affliction, then thou wilt hear and help. And now, behold, the children of Ammon and Moab and mount Seir, whom thou wouldest not let Israel invade, when they came out of the land of Egypt, but they turned from them,

and destroyed them not; Behold, I say, how they reward us, to come to cast us out of thy possession, which thou hast given us to inherit. O our God, wilt thou not judge them? For we have no might against this great company that cometh against us; neither know we what to do: but our eyes are upon thee.'"

Standing on the Word of God, we sought to face the whole Congolese government and the military that was backing them in the North. After my husband had talked at length with all the officials, the government decided to do an inquest. We believed that they were speaking in truth when they said that they had no knowledge of what was going on in the northern region.

The seven men who counseled the President were not only from the North, but we knew most of them personally and members of their families were among the believers in the local church. We listened to the radio daily. Even in the night we would turn the radio on to see if there was added news on what was happening among the churches. We knew that every church was under attack. Everyone feared that the missionaries would be forced to leave. Although we were not able to have open meetings at the church, we were able to get messages around to all the believers to pray and weep before the Throne of God. More than seven people were not allowed to gather in any one place, so everything was done discreetly.

The inquest was finally completed after six months and the Communist government ordered the local commander to reopen the church doors all over the area. The commander had lied about our church being a sect and he had taken the responsibility upon himself to close the doors without receiving permission from the President. God used this greedy military commander to change the course of the ministry. He was told to open the doors immediately and hold an official ceremony. With shaking hands, he stood before the huge church doors and with a crowbar, he reopened them. They had been closed by breaking up pews and nailing them to the doors.

A shout of victory went up as Gene and the Congolese Christians surged forward to enter and clean the place of worship that had been closed so long. The victory belonged to God. His might and power were evidenced before the whole population. The local military regime, that had been harassing God's people and all the villagers, had been dealt a deadly blow. What happened next was only another sign that God was for us and it was He who would stand against the enemy. The military commander lost his rank and was sent to Brazzaville to do some meaningless work behind an old desk in the corner of a government building.

Five other men joined him in trying to close the mission work, so they, too, were sent elsewhere to lower paying jobs. Although the church continued to suffer under many harsh restrictions, we, at least, were able to carry on the work of preaching the Gospel. There were hard core communists who put our names on hit lists to be exterminated at some future time, God intervened each time and saved us from harm. Our pastors were threatened time and again, but they remained faithful to the Lord. We all had seen the marvelous workings of God and we could not deny that our Heavenly Father had power in Heaven and on earth. Even as God said to Abraham and Sarah, He said to us, "Is anything too hard for the Lord" (Genesis 18:14). As long as we were willing to look to Him for help and guidance, He would do everything else. He had never failed us at any time. This experience served to keep us from turning and leaving the work during a most difficult time. As God had walked with the children of Israel through the desert wanderings, He was walking with us.

WILL YOU DIE FOR JESUS?

Before our return to the Congo in 1975, the church doors remained closed due to the local government decree. The national pastors were growing restless and tired of the restrictions that had been placed upon them. While praying together, several of them decided that if they went several hundred miles up river and way back into the villages of the deep jungle, they would be able to preach without hindrance. The trip was carefully planned and no one knew of their destination as they got into the dugout canoe and headed north on the great Ubangui River.

After several days, they arrived at the large village of Betou where we had a Congolese pastor and a large growing work. Back, along the Central African Republic border, the pastor had started many, many small churches. He and the Christians of that local church often walked to the end village deep in the forest. Along the way, the Word was taught and hundreds were added to the church of Jesus Christ. Pastor Edouard often rode his moped. This moped was supplied by Christians in this country. He was able to go more often and reach more people. But now, due to the church closings, he was not able to do anything and was watched very closely. He did not accompany Pastor Mowawa and a Bible school student as they took off for the interior along the forest paths. After a full

193

day of walking around stagnant, green pools of water and climbing over fallen trees, they arrived at the village of Bete Koumba. The Christians were ecstatic to see one of their pastors and quickly made plans to have services the next day.

The morning dawned sunny and beautiful. It was the perfect day to share Jesus with the Christians who were hungry for the Word of God. The village people had built their own mud church. It was always a highlight when a pastor came and they could sing and learn more about walking with Jesus. At the appointed time, the church began filling up. Every seat on the pole benches was taken. The Bible school student led the music while Pastor Mowawa sat behind him and waited for his turn to open the Lingala Bible and share God's message for the people. His message was, "Are you willing to die for Jesus?" Every eye was on him and there was silence that was broken only by the bleating of the sheep passing by or the many tropical birds high in the palm trees. Pastor Mowawa felt a jerking on his shirt.

The Bible school student in back of him suggested that he pause a moment and look outside the mud church. A strange feeling came over him as his eyes looked out to a group of militia surrounding the church. Without another word, he told the militia that if they wished to talk with him, he would gladly talk but first he wanted to finish his message. He returned to stand behind the roughly hewed pulpit and continued the message that God had given him. He ended with a prayer of dedication for the people before him, that they would stand fast in a day of godlessness and in a dark period of time when the church was being persecuted. All outside heard the message. The leader of the militia stepped forward and asked the two pastors to stand outside the church.

Slowly, Pastor Mowawa and Pascal walked a few feet away from the church. They were told that they had disobeyed the government's order and that they were preaching when they had no rights to do this or be in this village. The militia group began circling the pastors and their guns were pointed toward them. Without hesitation, the women of the church quickly walked through the militia and encircled the men of God. They joined their hands and stood fast. They defied the military and told them that if they were going to kill their pastors, they would also have to kill them. Many of these women were mothers, sisters and aunts of these young and arrogant military. Would they really shoot their own family members?

The women further said that they would not leave the pastors until the military promised to let the pastors depart in peace. After a short meeting, the militia agreed to let them go. The pastors departed and rejoiced on the long walk back to the river village of Betou. It reminded us of the Disciples who were imprisoned and let go. They didn't run and hide but they went on their way rejoicing and continuing to teach God's Word. After their arrival at the office of the river village, the local military man who knew them, told them to go on their way out the back door of the office where their dugout was tied.

On October 19, when the doors of all the churches were reopened, the churches grew more than ever and many were sharing their faith in Christ. When the President of our Mission arrived, they even asked him to send out more missionaries. How could this be that these men who were goose stepping to the tune of Communism and raising their fists in the air would ask for more missionaries? Had they seen something in our lives and in the lives of our pastors that they knew was real? Even though the official papers never ceased to come into our office and that of the church, we were given access to the whole territory to "preach the good news" as they put it. Yes, God's power was out in the open for all to see, and some were taking notice.

Five years passed by and the incident was almost forgotten. We received a letter from pastor Edouard at Betou, 125 miles from our station. We were excited to go and see the work that God was blessing in such an abundant way. We had many meetings and several choirs sang to prepare the hearts of the people for the baptism that was going to take place.

We walked down to the river's edge and entered a dugout where we could see the whole baptismal service. We could also take a lot of pictures of those who had decided to turn their backs on the village customs and fetishes and follow Jesus. Pastor Edouard and Pascal stood in the water and looked up at the throng of people on the bank. There were Muslims, government people and many villagers who came to see this event that was taking place. There were 31 who were dressed in white. One by one, they gave their testimony of what God had done in their lives. This was followed by the verse of a song and the pastors baptized them in the name of the Father, the Son and the Holy Spirit. As each one stepped out of the water, another Christian put a towel around the candidate and they walked up the embankment together.

The 31st candidate stepped into the water between the pastors. He looked up at the large crowd of people. Every eye was on him. As he began to talk, a hush came over all the people who were looking down at the men in the water. With much conviction, he began to speak in loud and distinct manner.

"All of you know who I am. Five years ago, I met these two pastors back in the jungle village of Bete Koumba. I was the leader of the militia and I ordered these men to leave the church and await their execution. They didn't run and they didn't even plead for their lives. They stood before us as men, men who didn't count their life as of any value. That day, I was willing to kill these two men for the Communist Party. Today, I am renouncing that life. These men that I hated, as well as my wife and the church, continued to pray for me and to love me. Those who I persecuted, I now love and they are willing to baptize me in the name of the Father, Son and Holy Spirit."

With these words, he was put beneath the water and came up with the sunshine of God's love on his face. The tears were streaming down our cheeks as we looked on in awe. God's Word was true. "And he that taketh not his cross, and followeth after me, is not worthy of me. He that findeth his life shall lose it: and he that loseth his life for my sake shall find it" (Matthew 10:38, 39).

Our labors for Christ were not in vain. Year after year as we taught young men in the Bible school, we often wondered how they would turn out. Would they remain

A crowd gathers at the river to see the militia leader baptized

faithful when we were gone or would they turn back to the life of the village? We had prayed for them and thousands of God's people had prayed, but the acid test would come when they were sent out alone. To us, they had now been tried and tested.

In Acts 15, the apostles and elders, with the whole church, decided to choose some of their own men to send to Antioch with Paul and Barnabas. They chose Judas and Silas, two men who were leaders among the brothers. In verses 25 and 26, we read, "It seemed good unto us, being assembled with one accord, to send chosen men unto you with our beloved Barnabas and Paul, men who have hazarded their lives for the name of our Lord Jesus Christ.

Our pastors had gone forth and risked their very lives for Christ. We have to ask ourselves if we are willing to do the same. Can our Lord count on the Christians of our present time, in this country, to stand for that which is righteous and holy and even to give our life for Him?

Socialism has once again returned to the Congo after a few years of total religious freedom. What will happen to the church in the coming days? We cannot answer that question, but we are sure that God will keep those who are His and He will preserve His Church for the Day of His return. Take note of that which has transpired at this present time in our own country and then listen to the timely Word of God. John 15:18, 19 "If the world hate you, ye know that it hated me before it hated you. If ye were of the world, the world would love his own: but because ye are not of the world, but I have chosen you out of the world, therefore the world hateth you."

PAPA JULES GOES HOME

Almost every child remembers the Bible story of Zacchaeus. He climbed a Sycamore tree just so that he would be able to see Jesus when he passed by. Zacchaeus was so very short that life was difficult for him, until he came face to face with the Lord Jesus. Jesus changed the whole course of his life because Zacchaeus placed his faith in the One who would change him from a thief to a follower.

It wasn't too long after we arrived at our jungle mission station that I became very much aware of a very short and skinny man who appeared to me to be Zacchaeus himself. He often took off in a trot to the village, to the church or out to his jungle garden. A few years went by and his wife died. He remarried and continued his daily treks to his garden to plant and to reap. When the church doors were open, Papa Jules was always there. If anything needed to be done, he would offer his help. He lived in a small but adequate mud hut that he called his home. It was his palace, a place that God often visited. Years passed by and there was never a time when Papa Jules slowed down—that is until he got a strange sore on his foot. Because he was so small, we didn't notice at first he was missing the church services on Sunday. Several more months passed before a family member came by the dispensary and told me that Papa Jules would like for me to come to his house for a visit.

In the late afternoon when the dispensary doors had been closed to the last sick person, I got on my moped and sped through the village until I came to Jules' home. Upon entering the hut, I smelled something very putrid. Jules' wife laid her hand on my arm and took me to his bedroom where he was sitting on a little stool hewed from soft wood. His foot was bandaged and his head was bowed low. The strength of his once strong body was gone and

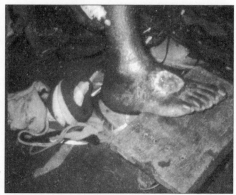

Papa Jules has large sore on his foot

his black skin seemed ashen in color. His head tilted a little and his eyes met mine. There was indescribable pain as he looked at me without speaking. Some of the pain came from not being productive any longer. He had been going to the small government hospital for help but they were not cleaning out the sores. This meant that when the antibiotics were injected, they were not effective. The bones in the foot were now exposed.

Tribal connections are very great and Jules was not from the area. Papa Jules was from a country north of Congo and he had no family but the family of God. Male nurses at the hospital knew this and refused to change the dressings on a daily basis. Over the years, we saw many die because no one at the hospital would take proper care of them due to the fact that the patient was not form the area or from their particular tribe or race. My heart grew heavier every day and I knew that somehow, I would have to enter the medical profession. Hundreds suffered and no one seemed to care, no compassion was manifest. The love of Jesus melted my heart when I gazed upon the suffering. The poor families had to provide a mattress for the hospital bed even though new ones had been issued. Who had taken them? So poor and yet they had to come up with money to buy medicines, food and a mosquito netting. Even with this, it didn't mean that the very ill patient would be cared for. The Government sent tons of medicine on the river boat, sheets, mattresses and sometimes food, but all this usually ended up in the hands of male nurses who worked in various old and broken down buildings of a decaying hospital. The name for all this was the corruption game and I fought it vigorously. Several mornings a week, I worked in the lab and sometimes in the operating room.

I could see why patients died. Antibiotics, bought by the family, were all too often pocketed and distilled water was injected into the patient. The vial of medicine in the hands of the nurse was then sold at half price to another ailing patient or exchanged for fish or dried monkey. I purposed in my heart to make a difference in the lives of the patients, even though I couldn't change the system of extreme corruption. Someday, God would give us a Christian hospital with a caring staff. I feared for Papa Jules. He needed to be in the hospital, but for what. Wasn't there anyone who would help him? His wife stated sadly that no one would approach him and meet his physical needs. Every day, I went to his home and changed the bandages. In reality, the foot needed to be amputated. It had to be severed above the ankle. Due to the fact that I had scheduled an amputation of a leper at the leprosy center, I did not have the time to make frequent visits to his home.

We had to fly down to the capital city of Brazzaville and get the medicine order that was coming in from West

Germany. We talked to the doctor at the hospital and asked him if he would be willing to do the amputation and take care of Jules until we returned from our trip. He agreed to do it to my face but I had a strange feeling that he would not be able to convince any of his nurses to do the work.

The plane arrived and we flew down to the capital. The time passed too quickly as I needed much time to get caught up on all the piles of old correspondence and type out a long form letter to all our faithful churches and supporters. While there, I worried about my many patients and especially, Jules. Would they have a change of heart and watch over him in the hospital? I had told the family to have someone stay at his bedside day and night and watch carefully when he was given an injection. They should monitor the nurse to make sure that the vial of medicine was actually put into the syringe and then injected into Jules.

We returned home to Impfondo on a Saturday. We had fourteen wonderful days of rest, fellowship and uninterrupted typing hours as well as time to buy food supplies for ourselves and the other missionaries. Everything was carefully packed and put on a riverboat for the trip north.

On a Monday morning, I walked into the hospital ward. The cot next to the very filthy wall had to be Jules' bed because it looked as if no one was in it. His wife sat on a little stool with her eyes closed in prayer. As I approached, she opened her eyes and they were filled with grief and tears. Jules was under a colored cloth and his head was turned toward the wall. All hope had turned to total despair. The wife related how the doctor had amputated the leg all the way to the thigh, but the nurses refused to come and change the dressings every day. They had insisted that Mrs. Thomas would take care of everything when

she returned home. The only problem with that theory
was that clean dressings couldn't wait for two full weeks.
They needed to be changed once or even twice a day.
Infection was rampant and the buttocks was now being
eaten away like a cancer. Papa Jules turned and his glazed
eyes looked at mine for a little ray of hope. Together, we
closed our tear filled eyes and we pleaded for God's help
and mercy. Deep in my heart, I knew that his days on this
earth were coming to an end. Taking his wife to one side,
I told her to gather his few things and her cooking pots
and I would return to the Mission to get my husband. He
would be able to carry Jules from the hospital bed to the
truck and take him to his village home.

Why did life seem so harsh? Why was there such a
thing as tribalism and hate. We saw no compassion and
love in that place. Tribalism in a hospital dictated
whether or not a person lived. Only Jesus could change
the hearts of those who discriminated in such an ugly
manner. These age old teachings seemed to be set in stone
and the little children learned early who they should trust
and who they should spurn.

At evening time, my husband and I got into the truck
and bumped along the muddy road. A little lantern was
lit by the bedside of Jules. Gene gathered Papa Jules in his
arms and laid him on a soft foam rubber mattress in the
back of the truck. Instead of returning to his house, the
family told us to take him to a compound of about four
houses. In the midst of these was a little mud hut. The
Christians in that compound were from his country of
the Central African Republic. They were faithful to God
and those who cared deeply about the sick and afflicted
in their midst. Each day, I drove to the little structure,
changed his dressings and then prayed for God's Presence
to be manifest in their midst. Jules no longer carried on a
conversation with anyone. His fever was high. Soon, he

would leave this world behind.

On a bright Saturday morning, I took Therese, a nurse who worked with me at the dispensary. We sat in silence as we slowly passed the many dilapidated mud houses. After a few turns on the muddy road, we came to Jule's small mud hut. As we cut away the soaked bandages, a small crowd gathered at the narrow, open door. My heart was overwhelmed with grief. It seemed so unfair that this little Zacchaeus type man had been treated so badly at the government hospital. Was there no justice anywhere? Therese and I worked several hours to clean away the rotting flesh and make him comfortable. His faithful wife took his hands in hers. Sadly, I watched the tears slipping down his drawn face. In that moment, I made a crucial decision that I had never made before and probably would not make again any time soon. I asked that his wife and Therese put their hands on mine as I gently put my hands on Jules. Weeping openly, I prayed and asked God to show His mercy and take Jules home to Heaven. He had suffered so much and far too long. He needed to rest awhile in the arms of Jesus. Christians in the open doorway obscured the sunlight with their bodies, but they were joining us in prayer with tear stained faces. Finishing my prayer, I pleaded with our Heavenly Father to carry this little man unto Himself. As I said, "Amen," I looked down at his peaceful face. Through the wet tears came a smile. He breathed very deeply and was gone. The great Presence of God was in our midst. He had answered prayer. Though the mud hut was small and dismal, it had been transformed into a place where God met His people. His glory shone and His power was evidenced by all who stood as witnesses. Not a person spoke as we rose up to leave in the Land Rover. The beautiful part was yet to come.

The funeral would be performed as soon as the wooden

casket was put together in the carpenter shed. Together, the whole church would gather, not in mourning, but in songs and praises that Jules had left his suffering and had entered into his reward. A very faithful servant had entered into his rest and would soon walk the streets of Glory.

Over the years, we, or the national pastors, would reside over many, many funerals. Some had lived out a long life, in African standards, and others left far too early. Because God helped us to be faithful in this difficult field, we would continue to lay to rest many who knew Him and thousands more who had not accepted Jesus as Savior. The jungle grave sites were many and it wouldn't be long until the rains came and the vines would cover over them. The beautifully cut cemeteries of America were nowhere to be found. In time, the jungle foliage would erase its hidden treasures, treasures that would only be known to God. Each child of God had left a hard life lived out through their earthly house, but they would dwell in a mansion high in the Heavens above.

Jesus gave us hope when He spoke with his Disciples. Jesus assured us in John 14:1-4, 6, "Let not your heart be troubled: ye believe in God, believe also in me. In my Father's house are many mansions: if it were not so, I would have told you, I will come again, and receive you unto myself, that where I am, there ye may be also. And whither I go, ye know, and the way ye know. I am the way, the truth and the life: no man cometh unto the Father, but by me." Jesus was explaining that a religion of good works was not enough for us to enter into Heaven. He made it very clear that Jesus is the only way that we have Eternal Life in Heaven.

So many in the world today want to bypass God's plan, by becoming a church member or just being baptized. Although these things are wonderful, we can only look at the thief on the cross beside Jesus. He was neither a church member nor was he baptized, but he did confess that Jesus was the Christ and Jesus told him that that day he would be in Paradise with Him. Believing in the Son and acknowledging Him as Savior and Lord will bring us into the family of God. No one else can make that choice for us. The choice is ours alone and we can do that today. Hebrews 3:7 "So, as the Holy Spirit says: Today, if you hear His voice, do not harden your hearts . . ."

WAR IN THE LAND

Eyes were fixed on us as we descended the airplane steps. Two lines of military were standing at attention with guns poised and machine gun shells in necklace type forms hanging around their necks. Something was radically wrong. Looking to the top of the airline buildings were many soldiers ready to fire at a given command.

Inside the building, we were taken to little stalls and body searches were made. No one seemed happy and everyone was tense. Perspiration ran down the soldiers

Some of the military is lined up at the airstrip

who were in heavy military fatigues. A military man spotted us. God knew that we needed a friend to help us through customs so that we would not have to pay. Our fluency in the language also gained a little attention and immediate respect. Home in the U.S. was now thousands of miles behind us and it was evident that we were going to face many new obstacles. Once outside the building, we were again confronted with a small regiment of fighting men. Beyond them under the shade of the trees were a number of enormous army tanks. The country seemed ready for war.

The communist government had been defeated at the polls for the first time in almost three decades. The former dictator was so sure that he would win that he allowed foreign observers to come and oversee the voting. The people had had enough bloodshed and misery and they were ready to take on Democracy. The new president had taken office but not without controversy. The two tribes of the south, the Lari Tribe and the Nibolek Tribe

A large Protestant church peppered with tank shells in Brazzaville

had lived more or less at peace for a hundred years or more, but the Laris felt that they were more intelligent and should hold the reins of the country. There was work to be done and we had no time at the moment to be bothered with tribal problems even though it was unsettling to see such a heavy military presence all over the city. It was our last term of service in the Congo. Our joyful years of serving the Lord in the jungle north were completed and it was now time to move on to establishing new churches in the capital city.

After finding a two story home to rent a mile or so from the center of Brazzaville, we settled in and asked God to guide us in starting some house churches. Old friends took us to various areas of the city where people were anxious for us to come and have Bible classes. The seven house churches were an immediate success. A young evangelist who lived near us heard about what we were doing and came to ask if he might aid in the many classes. The task was almost too much for one person to travel all over the city to have so many classes and the fact that God was sending helpers gave us a sense that our Heavenly Father was guiding us through these primary stages.

The Congolese evangelist invited us to his home so that we could lay the groundwork for reaching the city for Christ. This young man had once been the head of a rock music group and he was well known by the youth in the area. This alone would prove vital to us in the days ahead, as well as a hindrance.

Sitting in our Astro Van with the air conditioning on, we enjoyed working on the strategies that would help us to make inroads into the religious community where the liberal churches had a grip on the population. We knew that we would not be welcomed with open arms since we had already sensed hostility from some of those groups.

As we talked, several men in military garb approached the van and motioned for us to roll the windows down. They had previously been sitting on a seven-foot wall that surrounded the house, but we paid no attention to them as they seemed to be rather idle. This time, they were gruff and insolent. They asked our purpose and we explained what we were doing. With anger and authority, they asked us to leave and not come back. Looking at the evangelist, we asked for an explanation. He explained to us that the new president was from the Nibolek Tribe and that the people in this part of Brazzaville were from the Lari Tribe and trouble was brewing between them. We returned to the house and realized that we were living in the wrong area of Brazzaville. The Government that was in charge was looked at as an enemy in this part of the town. This Lari Tribe was numerous and quite able to cause much trouble for the present administration. We were hoping and praying that all this friction would pass.

Several years passed and the war clouds were gathering. The house churches had grown considerably all over the city and God was doing a great work in their midst. People were studying the Bible with study books entitled, "The Formation of the Disciple" that had been translated from English into French. The joys and blessings of the people were incalculable as they anticipated each class to begin.

Satan is never content when the Word of God is bearing fruit. Through any means, he will snatch away the seed that has been planted.

Night hours were increasingly turned into sounds of small arms fire. We often sat up in bed, listened and returned to sleep. What we heard would send the chills up and down our spines. Army trucks were patrolling the streets. Small branches in the trees would be broken off as bullets zinged through them. Was this a precursor to something greater than a squabble between the two tribes?

Each new day brought unusual sights. Slowly, large Chinese carts passed the house loaded to the top with furniture and other personal supplies. Upon questioning our house help, gardeners and night guards, we learned that the Nibolek Tribe was moving out of the area. Some had been shot execution style in the night hours and there was a general feeling that mass murder was about to take place as retaliation.

While my husband was away having classes in another area of the city, I stood behind the drapes in an upstairs bedroom and looked down upon the street that was crowded with people fleeing toward the four lane boulevard. That was the only street that led out of our area and to the center of the city. Young men were pushing the Chinese style pushcarts and mothers were pulling little children down the center of the street. Without warning, bullets began flying in the air just above the heads of the ever growing crowd. The fleeing people fell to the blacktop. Others hid behind the many trees that lined the street. My eyes were fixed on an old grandma who approached the eight foot wall that surrounded our two story house. In her flight, she stopped suddenly, placed the palms of her hands on our whitewashed wall. I could hear her praying in a very loud voice. "Heavenly Father, I do not know who lives in this house, but you know. Whoever they are, please keep and protect them." She hurried on. What did she know that we didn't know? We were soon to learn. Early evening was approaching and I went outside to await my husband. Through the steel gates, I looked down the road to the boulevard. I saw the red Astro Van as it turned onto our street. My heart froze in fear as I listened to the bullets that were being shot just a foot or so above his van. Tears were streaming down my face as he turned into the driveway. The night guard opened the steel gates and the van came into the carport. Gene was immediately alarmed as he saw me crying. After asking him if he knew that the shells were just clearing the van by a foot or so, he said that he did not know because he had the tape deck on loud as well as the air conditioner. He was listening to the beautiful song, "You are My Hiding Place." It was taken from David's song in Psalm 32:7 when he declared, "You are my hiding place; you will protect me from trouble and surround me with songs of deliverance."

There was a knock at the back door. One of our young men from church stood there breathing in gasps. He had come through the gully a short distance in back of our house. He had news that an offensive was being planned and there would be much trouble. The military, under the leadership of the new President and the Nibolek Tribe would be shelling our area. Americans who lived down the street from us and who worked for the American Embassy had already been evacuated in bullet proof Embassy cars. They had not bothered to warn us of the offensive. The days that followed would turn ugly and we would find ourselves in the midst of an ugly war that we could not escape from.

The heavy tanks rumbled by the outside wall. The army was in charge of shooting anyone who looked like a rebel from the Lari Tribe. As the ground rumbled and shook, the alarm from the van went off and the air was filled with its many shrill sounds. Looking out the upstairs windows, I could see the turrets of the tank swinging around in the middle of the street. As I screamed, Gene looked for the keys to turn off the van alarm system. Half way down the steps, he pointed the alarm button toward the direction of the car. The alarm fell silent and our hearts did, too. The tank turret was pointing directly at our house. It wasn't lost on us that the huge tank could have destroyed our wall and house in minutes. Sitting on the floor in the hallway, we were protected by two walls of brick and cement. Trembling from fear, we remembered that God was looking down upon us. Chapters from the book of Psalms sprang to life. With shells bursting all around us, we read these words in Psalm 33:13-19a "The Lord looketh from Heaven; He beholdeth all the sons of men. From the place of His habitation He looketh upon all the inhabitants of the earth. He fashioneth their hearts alike; He considereth all their works. There is no king saved by the multitude of a host: a mighty man is not delivered by his great strength. A horse is a vain thing for safety: neither shall he deliver any by his great strength. Behold, the eye of the Lord is upon them that fear Him, upon them that hope in His mercy; To deliver their soul from death . . ."

When only small gun fire could be heard, we went to bed. Throughout the night, we would awaken to hear cries of help from the street below. After endless turning and listening, we fell asleep.

Morning light revealed that we had no electricity. As my husband sat reading the Word by the French doors, I called to him from upstairs. He quickly left his chair and ascended the cement steps. We stood together behind the drapes and watched as a new truck and small Suzuki car approached and stopped in front of our house. The vehicles were undoubtedly stolen, as our Suzuki had been in those recent days. Bodies of dead soldiers had been piled up across the street from our home and it looked as if they were going to take them away. We had called the army general, a friend of ours, concerning the bodies and he assured us that they would remove the corpses. However, there were not the general's men in the street. They were from the opposition forces. I remained behind the drapes but my husband moved closer to the window to listen to their shouting. First, they shot in the air to make sure that no one came to observe them. Then they proceeded to make a line and throw the nude bodies from one to the other until the last one heaved them into the truck. One man happened to look up to our window and unfortunately, Gene was standing in open view.

A rebel soldier yelled to his leader to look up. As guns were now focused on our front bedroom window, the leader yelled for Gene to come down. He walked slowly to the stairs and started down. Our lives were now in jeopardy. The leader was very agitated and as I watched the scene unfold from upstairs, he jumped, reached the top of the wall and swung himself over to the yard below. By this time, Gene was slowly moving along the hallway downstairs. By the hand of God, he was stopped dead in his tracks. At that split second, the French doors were being bombarded with rapid gun fire. The chair in which he had been sitting was shot through six times and other shells were embedded in the dining room wall, just missing the china closet.

When the shooting subsided, Gene proceeded out the back kitchen door to the court yard and around to the front of the house where the rebel captain was standing. He was yelling in French, "Who lives in this house?" My husband explained that we lived there. He asked who lived upstairs and again my husband tried to explain that we did. At that point, the captain asked for money. When my husband pulled out five hundred francs from his pocket, the man became hot with anger. He wanted to know if he was only worth such a meagerly amount of money. By this time, Gene was also getting upset with the man because he was asking for at least a thousand dollars to take away the dead men. We then knew that the men were really rebels. God led him to tell the rebel that he was a pastor and had lived over forty years in the Congo and that nothing of this sort had ever happened to us. The man was stopped in his tracks as if someone had hit him. He repeated, "You are a pastor?" Gene said, "Yes, I am pastor Thomas." As the man had come over the walls, the front steel gate was still closed with a heavy steel lock. Looking as if he were a caged animal, he pleaded that the gate be opened and that he should be allowed to leave. He hurried across the street, entered the truck and sped away.

A week went by before men came from the electric company to fix the wires so that we might have electricity. Gene had to get permission from the army to drive the van out and then return with the men to fix the wires. As the lights came on, we saw the marvels of God. Metal from the bullets that had blasted the door had made small holes in the lamp beside the chair. In the hall where God had stopped Gene from proceeding into the living room, there were notches in the wall a quarter of an inch from where he stood. God had saved his life. One shell had split and it was buried in the broken cement of the wall. Yes, "The angel of the Lord encampeth round about them that fear Him, and delivereth them" (Psalm 34:7).

At the midnight hour, the army commander called us. Years before, he had been a student in my husband's English class in the high school at Impfondo, hundreds of miles to the north of this terrible war. He advised us that our lives were in grave and immediate danger and that we were to move from the area as soon as possible. Not knowing how to proceed at this point, we turned to our Heavenly Father and asked for His wisdom and direction.

As we rounded the corner of the boulevard with our last load of furniture, we looked back. Houses and buildings were being blown up by the army. Bodies were littered along the road. The boulevard was being closed off and the people within the area, that we left behind, would die or starve to death. Crying from sheer exhaustion and sadness, I wondered what God had for us to do in a city that was slowly being destroyed by hate, useless killings and the destruction of two races. We would learn the answers to these tormenting questions in God's time after this war was finished and a civil war began. The real war and the testing of our true faith was yet to come. We cried out, "Our soul waiteth for the Lord: He is our help and our shield. For our heart shall rejoice in Him, because we have trusted in His holy name. Let thy mercy, O Lord, be upon us . . ." (Psalm 33:20-22).

28

GRANDMA'S SUBSTITUTE

Back in the 1800's, there was a pretty young woman, named Ida Elmer, who grew up in the rugged hills of Wisconsin. Ida had godly parents who daily trained her in the Word of God. They also planted in her eager heart a need to evangelize, not only her surroundings, but the world. The greatest desire of her heart was to go to Bible college and prepare herself for a lifetime of service for God.

However, times were difficult in that farming community and there was a family to feed and clothe and send to school. The years of hard labor moved by slowly, but the dreams in Ida's heart did not diminish. If anything, the dream burned itself deeper in her soul. She began pouring over old books and reading all the stories that she could find about the great missionaries to Africa, such as Livingston and other great men of vision. The more she read, the more her soul ached to bring Christ to a people she had never before seen, a people that knew nothing of Jesus' love.

In that particular time of our country, just eking out a living from the soil was a major endeavor for any family. To alleviate the extreme family pressures, young women often married too early and the cycle of hardship would continue. Young Ida fell into that category.

217

Marriage seemed a way out of large family suffering that was due in part to the great depression. Most of the time, the misery turned into heartache as she busied herself with the daily chores of a very young family of her own. Raising six children from birth to adulthood would sure-ly need every ounce of strength and courage that she could muster up. Happiness was only a dream. Her husband, like so many others of that era, was a hard worker and a good provider, but was also harsh and unsympathetic. Deep in his heart, he undoubtedly longed for a better life, too. That better life would escape him and never be realized.

Sandy's Grandmother

The six children grew up and went into the world to make a living for themselves. Again, she found herself alone, just as she had been when she first married. The years had taken their toll on her husband. He busied himself with a few cows and other animals. He never entered into the things of God. He was even less interest-ed in entertaining ideas of some sort of missionary endeavor. He considered his wife a dreamer as she spoke of far away lands and strange peoples without a knowl-edge of God's love.

As the sun was setting over the nearby hills, Ida would take out her well worn Bible and sit in the worn rocking chair. This chair had soothed all her children during times of illness and during times when they were just plain hurting. She laid her head back against the faded pillow and closed her eyes. Her hair, wound in a top knot, had early on turned gray. Silence filled the room. The big grandfather's clock chimed as dusk fell upon the valley. Alone in the semi darkness, the tears began running down her cheeks. She recalled how her Heavenly Father had placed such a burning desire in her heart for Africa.

In the darkness, she felt God speaking again to her inner heart. He was saying to her, "Ida, it is true that you cannot go to Africa as a missionary at this late time in your life, but you can pray for a substitute."

Ida sat upright and opened her eyes. Immediately, she was filled with such joy that she could hardly contain it. God was actually giving her a way to go to Africa through the life of someone else. But who would that someone be? In the days that followed, she prayed a great deal each day. She sought the face of God and sang His praises concerning this new possibility. She was convinced that if God wanted her to send a substitute, He would show her who that person might be. God had laid out His plan and He alone would reveal it to her.

Many miles away in another farming community, her son, Robert, and his wife, Ella, were working hard to make a living for themselves and their two daughters. One afternoon, the youngest daughter was sitting in the grass watching an occasional car or truck pass by. Sometimes, it was a group of horses pulling farm machinery to be used in the fields. Very quietly, there was a bright Presence that surrounded the little five-year-old. The thin, pony tailed child got up from the grass and ran to her mother exclaiming, "Mommy, mommy, I am going to serve Jesus someday in a far away land!"

The young girl did not comprehend what had transpired. The family lived some distance from the city and it was a rare and wonderful occasion when the family could get into the new Model T Ford and go to Sunday school and church in the city. The family's knowledge of the Scriptures was quite rudimentary to say the least. There were no family devotions and no discussions about the individual spiritual needs of the soul.

After this experience, Ida began asking for Robert's youngest child to spend the summer with her. The beautiful garden provided much food. The trees and bushes gave forth fruit to make a lot of jam and jelly. Grandma enjoyed her little helper as they filled the big and little jars with vegetables, apples and peaches.

Pickles were stored in Ida's special brine and then stored in the fruit cellar. Being part of this was a special privilege. The jars were marked and put on the wood shelves. This labor of love reminded everyone that an abundant supply of food would be had for the harsh winter months ahead of them.

After the long toil of each day, there were times to sit under the tall, white trees that surrounded the storybook type home. Eating Ida's special cookies and drinking fresh milk from the cows was a real treat. The bees buzzed around the many flowers and the warm wind blew through the firs to create a special kind of enchantment for the lazy days of summer. Ida sat back in her rocking chair. She looked so old and tired now. The young child sat at her feet and relaxed before a very gentle handmaid of the Lord. She reached for the worn, family Bible that lay close to the rocker. Together, they read God's Word, memorized Scripture verses and sang songs. She taught the child to sing her first full song, "Wonderful Words of Life."

As the little girl grew, she and her sister, Maxine, sang at the many family gatherings. Due to numerous health problems in the young family, they moved south to southern Wisconsin. It wasn't hard to leave the hard life of farming. When the parents found employment in the city, this meant a better and more comfortable lifestyle.

Other things changed as well. The two sisters began attending an evangelical church in the city. They had been invited by two other sisters who were neighbors nearby. The sad little girl had a deep hunger in her heart for fellowship and love. She harbored these feelings within her like a well-guarded secret that was locked in the deep recesses of her heart, never to be shared with anyone who knew her. The teen years were soon upon the girl and Satan was there to entice her with all the thrills and excitement of this world. These thrills were like a magnet drawing her to the bright lights of the dancing halls. Yet, with all the glamorous appeal of the bright lights, Satan was not able to keep her from going to church every time the doors were open. Opportunities were available for her to use her voice in singing with the church trio and the choir. A loving, godly, church family gave her a solid foundation for her future life. After an almost fatal car accident, she was awakened within. The young girl heard a still small voice calling her from within saying, "These are the crossroads for you. You must now make your choice to follow me."

After falling before a Holy God at the church altar, she confessed her sins and her wayward walk in sinful pleasures and started on a new road. This new and sometimes frightening road would change the course of her life.

She had not thought of the world outside her own before, but for some strange reason, Africa came to mind. The church had missionaries in Cuba but no one had come to the church from the continent of Africa. Why was there such a compulsion to learn about the dark land, as it was called? The secret desire to learn about these strange lands and peoples became an obsession. The end result of this search revealed that God wanted her to go there as a missionary. Sharing this desire with family and friends brought mixed emotions and comments. Many felt that surely this girl couldn't be serious about such a plan. Without doubt, the whole thing would pass with time. Others thought that no one in their right mind would consider leaving the good life to go to a place that was noted, in books, as the missionary's graveyard. Also, there was idol worship, sacrifices, extreme poverty and many unusual diseases.

After being baptized, her testimony became clear. She didn't know how she would realize God's plan, she only knew what God wanted her to do. God does not repent of His calling. From the beginning of Genesis to this present time, God has made a place in His vineyard for His own. God's candidate was ready to go and I was that candidate. Before the whole church, I stood and declared, "I was that little pigtailed girl chosen by God to be a missionary to Africa. Ida Elmer Wacker with the top knot and gray hair was my grandmother. She couldn't go herself, but she could go through me. I was to be her substitute."

Grandma lived to be almost a hundred years of age and she delighted in the Lord that He should allow her to stay on this earth long enough to see her prayers answered. Returning from Africa, we saw her bedridden and blind. I would never see her again on this earth, but I felt that bond that was between us because she had been faithful in praying for me that I might have a part in winning people and treating the multitudes that were not only sick because of sin, but dying because of their diseases.

Others have been called down through the ages, perhaps in more dramatic ways, and for much greater tasks, such as calling a nation unto God, but the call in itself remains the same. Isaiah was a great example of how God calls his people to serve Him. "In the year that king Uziah died, I saw also the Lord sitting upon a throne, high and lifted up, and his train filled the temple. Above it stood the seraphim: each one had six wings; with twain he covered his face, and with twain he covered his feet, and with twain, he did fly. And one cried unto another, and said, Holy, holy, holy, is the Lord of hosts: the whole earth is full of His glory. And the posts of the door moved at the voice of Him that cried, and the house was filled with smoke." Then said I, "Woe is me! For I am undone; because I am a man of unclean lips, and I dwell in the midst of a people of unclean lips: for mine eyes have seen the King, the Lord of hosts. Then flew one of the seraphim unto me, having a live coal in his hand, which he had taken with the tongs from off the altar! And he laid it upon my mouth, and said, Lo, this hath touched thy lips; and thine iniquity is taken away, and thy sin purged. Also, I heard the voice of the Lord, saying, Whom shall I send, and who will go for us? Then said I, Here am I; send me. And he said, "Go and tell this people" (Isaiah 6:1-9a).

God's vineyard is the world. The Church of Christ must send workers or substitutes to the whole earth to proclaim the Good News that Jesus saves. Grandma's intercessory prayers and God's appointment sent me to Africa. You also can pray faithfully and send out a multitude to the far flung reaches of a world dying for lack of hope, love and the Savior. The jungle walls were so far reaching that they seemed to go on without end. The task that God sent my husband and me to do appeared too great—and it was. But, what we couldn't do in ourselves, God did through us. The little handful of people, who made up the first church, started to grow and grow. That church was like a seed multiplying before our eyes. God blessed His Word even as He did for the early church in the book of Acts. Through much persecution and because of a Communistic government, many of God's people became stronger in their faith. In the end, a national church emerged to carry on where the missionaries left off. They are now paddling the dugout canoes along the serpentine rivers to reach their own people. The once very dark jungle has light shining in it as the God of hope has penetrated the hearts and lives of the large Pygmy population as well. Thousands of forest people, who live and exist unnoticed by the rest of mankind, are turning from Paganism to Christ. Many have passed on before their time. When Jesus comes again, the deep jungle will give up its many graves, graves that cannot be seen because of the vines and overgrowth. They, too, will hear the trumpet sound and their existence will be remembered no more. Our Heavenly Father will open the gates of Glory that they might enter into their rest. No longer will they sleep on pole beds to languish in pain and fever from malaria, nor will they have to trudge the miles of muddy, jungle trails to search for food to keep them alive one more day. In His Kingdom, they will walk the streets of gold in the New Jerusalem. The songs of death in the village will be heard no more. A new song will be given to them as they join their voices with all God's people to sing the Hallelujah chorus with the angels on high. They will live in His presence forever and ever.

"O sing unto the Lord a new song: sing unto the Lord, all the earth. Sing unto the Lord, bless His name; show forth His salvation from day to day. Declare His glory among the heathen, His wonders among all the people" (Psalm 96:1-3).

The jungle walls of northern Congo are still there, but God has called others to penetrate them and continue the difficult task of seeking out the lost ones. As a new generation of children has been born, God is looking for more workers to stand in the gap. God may be calling you. Heed the call!